VISUAL J++™
FOR
DUMMIES®

Quick Reference

by Namir Clement Shammas

IDG BOOKS ™
WORLDWIDE

IDG Books Worldwide, Inc.
An International Data Group Company

Foster City, CA ✦ Chicago, IL ✦ Indianapolis, IN ✦ Southlake, TX

Visual J++™ For Dummies® Quick Reference

Published by
IDG Books Worldwide, Inc.
An International Data Group Company
919 E. Hillsdale Blvd.
Suite 400
Foster City, CA 94404
www.idgbooks.com (IDG Books Worldwide Web site)
www.dummies.com (Dummies Press Web site)

Library of Congress Catalog Card No.: 97-80122

ISBN: 0-7645-0253-0

Printed in the United States of America

10 9 8 7 6 5 4 3 2 1

1P/SS/QY/ZX/IN

Distributed in the United States by IDG Books Worldwide, Inc.

Distributed by Macmillan Canada for Canada; by Transworld Publishers Limited in the United Kingdom; by IDG Norge Books for Norway; by IDG Sweden Books for Sweden; by Woodslane Pty. Ltd. for Australia; by Woodslane Enterprises Ltd. for New Zealand; by Longman Singapore Publishers Ltd. for Singapore, Malaysia, Thailand, and Indonesia; by Simron Pty. Ltd. for South Africa; by Toppan Company Ltd. for Japan; by Distribuidora Cuspide for Argentina; by Livraria Cultura for Brazil; by Ediciencia S.A. for Ecuador; by Addison-Wesley Publishing Company for Korea; by Ediciones ZETA S.C.R. Ltda. for Peru; by WS Computer Publishing Corporation, Inc., for the Philippines; by Unalis Corporation for Taiwan; by Contemporanea de Ediciones for Venezuela; by Computer Book & Magazine Store for Puerto Rico; by Express Computer Distributors for the Caribbean and West Indies. Authorized Sales Agent: Anthony Rudkin Associates for the Middle East and North Africa.

For general information on IDG Books Worldwide's books in the U.S., please call our Consumer Customer Service department at 800-762-2974. For reseller information, including discounts and premium sales, please call our Reseller Customer Service department at 800-434-3422.

For information on where to purchase IDG Books Worldwide's books outside the U.S., please contact our International Sales department at 415-655-3200 or fax 415-655-3295.

For information on foreign language translations, please contact our Foreign & Subsidiary Rights department at 415-655-3021 or fax 415-655-3281.

For sales inquiries and special prices for bulk quantities, please contact our Sales department at 415-655-3200 or write to the address above.

For information on using IDG Books Worldwide's books in the classroom or for ordering examination copies, please contact our Educational Sales department at 800-434-2086 or fax 817-251-8174.

For press review copies, author interviews, or other publicity information, please contact our Public Relations department at 415-655-3000 or fax 415-655-3299.

For authorization to photocopy items for corporate, personal, or educational use, please contact Copyright Clearance Center, 222 Rosewood Drive, Danvers, MA 01923, or fax 508-750-4470.

About the Author

Namir Clement Shammas is a full-time author who specializes in object-oriented programming and Windows programming books. He has written and coauthored more than 60 programming books, including *Object-Oriented Programming For Dummies, Visual C++ For Dummies Quick Reference,* and *Visual Basic 5 For Dummies Quick Reference* (all by IDG Books Worldwide, Inc.). Namir holds B.S. and M.S. degrees in chemical engineering.

ABOUT IDG BOOKS WORLDWIDE

Welcome to the world of IDG Books Worldwide.

IDG Books Worldwide, Inc., is a subsidiary of International Data Group, the world's largest publisher of computer-related information and the leading global provider of information services on information technology. IDG was founded more than 25 years ago and now employs more than 8,500 people worldwide. IDG publishes more than 275 computer publications in over 75 countries (see listing below). More than 60 million people read one or more IDG publications each month.

Launched in 1990, IDG Books Worldwide is today the #1 publisher of best-selling computer books in the United States. We are proud to have received eight awards from the Computer Press Association in recognition of editorial excellence and three from *Computer Currents'* First Annual Readers' Choice Awards. Our best-selling ...For Dummies® series has more than 30 million copies in print with translations in 30 languages. IDG Books Worldwide, through a joint venture with IDG's Hi-Tech Beijing, became the first U.S. publisher to publish a computer book in the People's Republic of China. In record time, IDG Books Worldwide has become the first choice for millions of readers around the world who want to learn how to better manage their businesses.

Our mission is simple: Every one of our books is designed to bring extra value and skill-building instructions to the reader. Our books are written by experts who understand and care about our readers. The knowledge base of our editorial staff comes from years of experience in publishing, education, and journalism — experience we use to produce books for the '90s. In short, we care about books, so we attract the best people. We devote special attention to details such as audience, interior design, use of icons, and illustrations. And because we use an efficient process of authoring, editing, and desktop publishing our books electronically, we can spend more time ensuring superior content and spend less time on the technicalities of making books.

You can count on our commitment to deliver high-quality books at competitive prices on topics you want to read about. At IDG Books Worldwide, we continue in the IDG tradition of delivering quality for more than 25 years. You'll find no better book on a subject than one from IDG Books Worldwide.

IDG BOOKS WORLDWIDE

John Kilcullen
CEO
IDG Books Worldwide, Inc.

Steven Berkowitz
President and Publisher
IDG Books Worldwide, Inc.

IDG Books Worldwide, Inc., is a subsidiary of International Data Group, the world's largest publisher of computer-related information and the leading global provider of information services on information technology. International Data Group publishes over 275 computer publications in over 75 countries. Sixty million people read one or more International Data Group publications each month. International Data Group's publications include: ARGENTINA: Buyer's Guide, Computerworld Argentina, PC World Argentina; AUSTRALIA: Australian Macworld, Australian PC World, Australian Reseller News, Computerworld, IT Casebook, Network World, Publish, Webmaster; AUSTRIA: Computerwelt Österreich, Networks Austria, PC Tip Austria; BANGLADESH: PC World Bangladesh; BELARUS: PC World Belarus; BELGIUM: Data News, BRAZIL: Annuário de Informática, Computerworld, Connections, Macworld, PC Player, PC World, Publish, Reseller News, Supergamepower; BULGARIA: Computerworld Bulgaria, Network World Bulgaria, PC & MacWorld Bulgaria; CANADA: CIO Canada, Client/Server World, ComputerWorld Canada, InfoWorld Canada, NetworkWorld Canada, WebWorld; CHILE: Computerworld Chile, PC World Chile; COLOMBIA: Computerworld Colombia, PC World Colombia; COSTA RICA: PC World Centro America; THE CZECH AND SLOVAK REPUBLICS: Computerworld Czechoslovakia, Macworld Czech Republic, PC World Czechoslovakia; DENMARK: Communications World Danmark, Computerworld Danmark, Macworld Danmark, PC World Danmark, Techworld Denmark; DOMINICAN REPUBLIC: PC World Republica Dominicana; ECUADOR: PC World Ecuador; EGYPT: Computerworld Middle East, PC World Middle East; EL SALVADOR: PC World Centro America; FINLAND: MikroPC, Tietoverkko, Tietoviikko; FRANCE: Distributique, Hebdo, Info PC, Le Monde Informatique, Macworld, Reseaux & Telecoms, WebMaster France; GERMANY: Computer Partner, Computerwoche, Computerwoche Extra, Computerwoche FOCUS, Global Online, Macwelt, PC Welt; GREECE: Amiga Computing, GamePro Greece, Multimedia World, GUATEMALA: PC World Centro America; HONDURAS: PC World Centro America; HONG KONG: Computerworld Hong Kong, PC World Hong Kong, Publish in Asia; HUNGARY: ABCD CD-ROM, Computerworld Szamitastechnika, Internetto online Magazine, PC World India, Publish in Asia; INDONESIA: InfoKomputer PC World, Komputek Computerworld, Publish in Asia; IRELAND: ComputerScope, PC Live!; ISRAEL: Macworld Israel, People & Computers/Computerworld; ITALY: Computerworld Italia, Macworld Italia, Networking Italia, PC World Italia; JAPAN: DTP World, Macworld Japan, Nikkei Personal Computing, OS/2 World Japan, SunWorld Japan, Windows NT World, Windows World Japan; KENYA: PC World East African; KOREA: Hi-Tech Information, Macworld Korea, PC World Korea; MACEDONIA: PC World Macedonia; MALAYSIA: Computerworld Malaysia, PC World Malaysia, Publish in Asia; MALTA: PC World Malta; MEXICO: Computerworld Mexico, PC World Mexico; MYANMAR: PC World Myanmar; NETHERLANDS: Computer! Totaal, LAN Internetworking Magazine, LAN World Buyers Guide, Macworld Netherlands, Net, WebWereld; NEW ZEALAND: Absolute Beginners Guide and Plain & Simple Series, Computer Buyer, Computer Industry Directory, Computerworld New Zealand, MTB, Network World, PC World New Zealand; NICARAGUA: PC World Centro America; NORWAY: Computerworld Norge, CW Rapport, Datamagasinet, Financial Rapport, Kursguide Norge, Macworld Norge, Multimediaworld Norge, PC World Ekspress Norge, PC World Nettverk, PC World Norge, PC World ProduktGuide Norge; PAKISTAN: Computerworld Pakistan; PANAMA: PC World Panama; PEOPLE'S REPUBLIC OF CHINA: China Computer Users, China Computerworld, China InfoWorld, China Telecom World Weekly, Computer & Communication, Electronic Design China, Electronics Today, Electronics Weekly, Game Software, PC World China, Popular Computer Week, Software Weekly, Software World, Telecom World; PERU: Computerworld Peru, PC World Profesional Peru, PC World SoHo Peru; PHILIPPINES: Click!, Computerworld Philippines, PC World Philippines, Publish in Asia; POLAND: Computerworld Poland, Computerworld Special Report Poland, Cyber, Macworld Poland, Networld Poland, PC World Komputer; PORTUGAL: Cerebro/PC World, Computerworld/Correio Informático, Dealer World Portugal, Mac*In/PC*In Portugal, Multimedia World; PUERTO RICO: PC World Puerto Rico; ROMANIA: Computerworld Romania, PC World Romania, Telecom Romania; RUSSIA: Computerworld Russia, Mir PK, Publish, Seti; SINGAPORE: Computerworld Singapore, PC World Singapore, Publish in Asia; SLOVENIA: Monitor; SOUTH AFRICA: Computing SA, Network World SA, Software World SA; SPAIN: Communications World Espana, Computerworld España, Dealer World España, Macworld España, PC World España; SRI LANKA: Infolink PC World; SWEDEN: CAP&Design, Computer Sweden, Corporate Computing Sweden, Internetworld Sweden, it.branschen, Macworld Sweden, MaxiData Sweden, MikroDatorn, Nätverk & Kommunikation, PC World Sweden, PCaktiv, Windows World Sweden; SWITZERLAND: Computerworld Schweiz, Macworld Schweiz, PCtip; TAIWAN: Computerworld Taiwan, Macworld Taiwan, NEW ViSiON/Publish, PC World Taiwan, Windows World Taiwan; THAILAND: Publish in Asia, Thai Computerworld; TURKEY: Computerworld Türkiye, Macworld Türkiye, Network World Türkiye, PC World Turkiye; UKRAINE: Computerworld Kiev, Multimedia World Ukraine, PC World Ukraine; UNITED KINGDOM: Acorn User UK, Amiga Action UK, Amiga Computing UK, Apple Talk UK, Computing, Macworld, Parents and Computers UK, PC Advisor, PC Home, PSX Pro, The WEB, UNITED STATES: Cable in the Classroom, CIO Magazine, Computerworld, DOS World, Federal Computer Week, GamePro Magazine, InfoWorld, I-Way, Macworld, Network World, PC Games, PC World, Publish, Video Event, THE WEB Magazine, and WebMaster; online webzines: JavaWorld, NetscapeWorld, and SunWorld Online; URUGUAY: InfoWorld Uruguay; VENEZUELA: Computerworld Venezuela, PC World Venezuela, and VIETNAM: PC World Vietnam. 3/24/97

Dedication

To a very special friend and CONTRA dance guru, Wayne Scank.

Author's Acknowledgments

This book is the fruit of the efforts of many people. I would like to thank IDG Books Worldwide, Inc. for sharing my vision in this book. Many thanks to my literary agent, Carol McLyndon of Waterside Productions, for encouraging me and pursuing this project. I also would like to thank the technical editor, Discovery Computing. Many thanks to the project editor, Kelly Ewing, and the copy editor, John Edwards. They have made valuable contributions to shaping this manuscript. Let's do it again!

Publisher's Acknowledgments

We're proud of this book; please send us your comments about it by using the IDG Books Worldwide Registration Card at the back of the book or by e-mailing us at feedback/dummies@idgbooks.com. Some of the people who helped bring this book to market include the following:

Acquisitions, Development, and Editorial

Project Editor: Kelly Ewing

Acquisitions Editor: Jill Pisoni

Copy Editor: John Edwards

Technical Editor: Discovery Computing, Inc.

Editorial Manager: Colleen Rainsberger

Editorial Assistant: Darren Meiss

Production

Project Coordinator: E. Shawn Aylsworth

Layout and Graphics: Cameron Booker, Linda M. Boyer, Angela F. Hunckler, Heather N. Pearson, Brent Savage

Proofreaders: Henry Lazarek, Christine Berman, Karen York

Indexer: Ty Koontz

Special Help: Stephanie Koutek, Proof Editor

General and Administrative

IDG Books Worldwide, Inc.: John Kilcullen, CEO; Steven Berkowitz, President and Publisher

IDG Books Technology Publishing: Brenda McLaughlin, Senior Vice President and Group Publisher

Dummies Technology Press and Dummies Editorial: Diane Graves Steele, Vice President and Associate Publisher; Judith A. Taylor, Product Marketing Manager; Kristin A. Cocks, Editorial Director; Mary Bednarek, Acquisitions and Product Development Director

Dummies Trade Press: Kathleen A. Welton, Vice President and Publisher

IDG Books Production for Dummies Press: Beth Jenkins, Production Director; Cindy L. Phipps, Manager of Project Coordination, Production Proofreading, and Indexing; Kathie S. Schutte, Supervisor of Page Layout; Shelley Lea, Supervisor of Graphics and Design; Debbie J. Gates, Production Systems Specialist; Robert Springer, Supervisor of Proofreading; Debbie Stailey, Special Projects Coordinator; Tony Augsburger, Supervisor of Reprints and Bluelines; Leslie Popplewell, Media Archive Coordinator

Dummies Packaging and Book Design: Patti Sandez, Packaging Specialist; Lance Kayser, Packaging Assistant; Kavish + Kavish, Cover Design

♦

The publisher would like to give special thanks to Patrick J. McGovern, without whom this book would not have been possible.

♦

Contents at a Glance

Table of Contents

How to Use This Book

You know, you're pretty smart for buying a ...*For Dummies Quick Reference* that covers Visual J++. I mean, like genius-level smart. You understand that all *you* need out of a book on Visual J++ is a few reminders about how those strange, convoluted codes work and the occasional simple example to get you started. After all, you're a programmer, and you don't need step-by-step instructions on using this language.

And you've got the right book in your hands. This book is not a step-by-step learning tool, but rather a reference tool for reminding yourself about how certain elements of Java work. You can keep this book by your computer or workstation and consult the book whenever you need a quick-fix of Java syntax.

How This Book Is Organized

This book is made up of 12 parts, each of which covers a specific element of Java programming, and a Glossary. The elements are organized alphabetically within each part. To find information about a program element, think about what classification it falls under and then look in the appropriate part. For example, to find out how to declare constants, look in "Part III: Constants and Variables," check under the heading "Constants," and *voilà!*

The parts of this book are organized by subject matter, as follows:

Part I: Getting to Know Visual J++: Jump right into this part if you want some background information on using Visual J++. Here's where I cover using the Developer Studio and compiling Java programs, among other subjects.

Part II: Editing and Debugging: This part covers the Developer Studio features that help you find and replace text as well as debug Java programs.

Part III: Constants and Variables: The title is pretty self-explanatory. Topics include using constants, variables, arrays, and predefined data types.

Part IV: Operators: Go to this part for information about the different kinds of operators (Boolean, relational, arithmetic, and the like).

Part V: Decision-Making Constructs: Good old-fashioned `if-then` and related statements are covered in this part. I also go into the complexities of the `switch` statement.

Part VI: Loops: Travel to the wonderful world of loops; visit the exciting `do-while` and `for` codes, see loops in their nests, and uncover the mysterious word *iterations*.

Part VII: Classes: I show you how to create classes, class hierarchies, abstract classes, and the components of a class. I also show you how to use exceptions to handle runtime errors.

Part VIII: Strings and Methods: I discuss how to declare and use the methods of a class. In addition, this part looks at the class `String` and offers a reference of its most commonly used methods to manipulate text.

Part IX: Handling the Mouse and Keyboard: I discuss the methods that allow you to manage using the mouse (clicking, moving, and tracking the mouse pointer). In addition, I discuss how to read keyboard input.

Part X: Basic Controls: This title says it all! I cover the basic visual controls that you can display on a Web page. These controls include labels, buttons, check boxes, and text fields.

Part XI: Scrollable Controls: I present the scrollable controls, which include the scrollbar and the list box. These controls allow you to select from a range of values or from a list of items.

Part XII: Advanced OOP: Look here to find out about working with dialog boxes, layout managers, and menus.

Glossary: Techie Talk: Every technical reference needs a good glossary, and this book is no exception. I did my best to provide you with definitions for all the strange verbiage that Java has to offer, and I threw in the meanings for a few general programming terms just for good measure.

Conventions Used in This Book

Individual code elements, such as variable names, appear in the text this way: myVariable. Often the code that I use as an example isn't just one or two lines, so you see something similar to the following:

```
class Rabbit
{
  protected double m_fXCoord; // X coordinate
  protected double m_fYCoord; // Y coordinate
  public void moveTo(double fnewXCoord,
                     double fnewYCoord);
  public void moveBy(double fXchange, double
    fYchange);
  public double getXCoord();
  public double getYCoord();
}
```

I also use italics in code to show that certain terms are used as placeholders and aren't really code. For example, you may see:

```
class className
```

The word className, which is a placeholder for the class name of your choice, is in italics to differentiate it from the word class, which is the actual syntax for the declaration.

Finally, be aware that I use *Hungarian notation* preceding the names of many program elements. These notations denote how the element is being used in the code block. Because I use a lot of Microsoft products, I prefer that company's loose version of Hungarian notation, such as *n* for integer; *f* for floating-point numbers (float and double); *u* for unsigned integer; *c* for character; *b* for Boolean; and *l* for long.

The Cast of Icons

I use marginal icons next to certain paragraphs throughout the various parts. When you see an icon, pay special attention to the text next to it. That text can make the difference between a good program that runs just fine and a debugging nightmare.

Text flagged with the Tip icon is super-useful information that saves you time or clarifies syntax.

Use paragraphs marked with the Fast Track icon to save yourself some programming time.

Notice that the Warning icon has a picture of a little bomb on it. Terrible things can happen if you disregard text marked with this icon. Trust me!

Occasionally I can't go into a lot of detail about a particular program element, so I include a cross-reference to the appropriate chapter in *Java For Dummies,* 2nd Edition, by Aaron E. Walsh (published by IDG Books Worldwide, Inc.) whenever necessary. This icon marks those references.

Whenver you want to know how to use a particular Visual J++ element, look for this icon.

Want an example of a Visual Basic element being used in a real-life program? Then look for this icon.

If you're an absolute beginner to the joys of Java programming, I suggest that you pick up a copy of *Visual J++ For Dummies,* by Michael I. Hyman (IDG Books Worldwide, Inc.) and peruse it at your leisure. That book goes into much more detail about the programming language than this one does — but you can't fit the big book in your hip pocket.

## Part 1

Getting to Know Visual J++

In this part, you discover the basics of working with the Developer Studio as the environment for using Visual J++. The various sections in this part show you how to edit and manage project files as well as how to create Java console applications and Java applets.

In this part

- ✓ Learning about the AWT library
- ✓ Finding out about the basic role of classes
- ✓ Working with console applications
- ✓ Finding out about the general parts of the Developer Studio
- ✓ Exiting Visual J++
- ✓ Getting help
- ✓ Using the Java Applet Wizard
- ✓ Creating applets in this book
- ✓ Using the JVIEW interpreter
- ✓ Working with projects
- ✓ Using project workspace
- ✓ Starting and exiting Visual J++
- ✓ Working with text files
- ✓ Using the toolbars
- ✓ Using the Workspace window

AWT Library

Java uses a number of external libraries to support creating sophisticated applications. Most noted is the AWT (Application Windows Toolkit) library. This library declares and makes available several classes that support a variety of visual controls such as labels, buttons, check boxes, radio buttons, list boxes, text fields, and so on. The latter parts of this book offer references for these visual controls and include the AWT classes that support these classes.

Classes

Whether you're a novice or veteran Java programmer, you have no doubt noticed that every .JAVA file contains the declaration of at least one class. *Classes* are units of programming that help you describe a category of objects. This description states what the object is made of (that is, its *attributes*) and what operations it performs or responds to (that is, its *methods*). For example, you can declare a class that represents a very basic window. This class would, for example, define the height, width, color, frame width, and frame color. The class would also contain methods to create, display, hide, minimize, and remove a window.

Classes are central to Java. When you program in Visual J++, you employ numerous classes already developed by other programmers for you. You also will write new classes that most likely will use the existing classes (such as the ones in the AWT library). For more information on declaring and using classes, see Part VII.

Console Applications

You can build two kinds of Java programs:

+ The first type is text-based (also called a *console application*). When you ask the Developer Studio to run this kind of program, it invokes the JVIEW interpreter. This utility displays a window that displays the output, and you can enter any required input.

+ The second type of program creates an applet that is typically used by a Web page. This kind of application uses the AWT (Application Windows Toolkit) library, which supports a graphical user interface.

The following is a simple Java program that is a console application. The program merely displays a greeting message.

```
import java.io.*;

class SayHi {
  public static void main(String args[]) {
    System.out.println("Hello World");
  }
}
```

To build this kind of program, first load the Developer Studio and then perform the following steps:

1. Choose File⇨New or press Ctrl+N to open a new file. The Developer Studio displays the New dialog box. This dialog box allows you to create a number of different files. Select the Projects page.

2. The Developer Studio displays the New dialog box. Select Java Project from the list of project types, and then type the project name **SayHi** in the Project name text box. Click the OK button when you're finished.

3. Choose File⇨New again. This time, select the Files page and click Java Source File from the list of files. Type **SAYHI.JAVA** in the File name text box and then click the OK button.

4. Type the source code that is shown preceding this list and save it as the file SAYHI.JAVA, using File⇨Save As. The Developer Studio opens the Save As dialog box. Type the filename and then click the Save button.

5. Choose Project⇨Add To Project⇨Files to insert the file SAYHI.JAVA in the SayHi project. The Developer Studio displays the Insert Files into Project dialog box. Type the source code filename and then click the Add button. The source code file now becomes part of the current project.

6. Select Project⇨Settings, and the Developer Studio displays the Project Settings dialog box. Click the Debug page and then click the button labeled Stand-alone interpreter. Type the name of the class file (for example, SayHi.class) in the text box labeled Class for debugging/executing. Finally, click the OK button to close this dialog box.

7. Choose Build⇨Execute SayHi or press Ctrl+F5. The Developer Studio displays a dialog box that asks whether you want to build the project files. Click the Yes button. The Developer Studio runs the program and displays the JVIEW interpreter in a DOS window (or command prompt, if you're using Windows NT), which contains the text `Hello World`. When the Developer Studio launches the JVIEW interpreter, it also automatically closes the DOS window after the program ends.

To compile any other console application, perform the previous steps while replacing the name SayHi with the name of the project.

When you run a console application from within the Developer Studio, the DOS window that runs the JVIEW interpreter closes when the program ends. You therefore have no time to examine the output. You can resolve this issue in three ways:

✦ Press Pause to pause the execution of the JVIEW interpreter. This approach can be tricky, because you must press the Pause key at exactly the right time. Press Enter to resume execution of the program.

✦ Insert the statement `import java.io.*;` at the beginning of the source code and insert the following source code at the end of the method `main()` to force the program to wait for you to press Enter:

```
try {
   int b = System.in.read();
}
catch(IOException e) {}
```

✦ Run a DOS session separately and execute the JVIEW interpreter. In this case, move to the directory that contains the project files and type the following command to execute the CLASS file:

```
jview myProject
```

Developer Studio

Microsoft has chosen to use a comment environment to develop applications for FORTRAN, Visual C++, and Visual J++. This environment is the Developer Studio, which you need to run in order to work with Visual J++ (or FORTRAN or Visual C++). The Developer Studio contains the following general components:

✦ **Project manager:** Supervises the files that are part of a programming project. A project has at least one .JAVA file. Typical Web-oriented projects have one or more .JAVA files and one or more .HTML files.

✦ **Editor:** Allows you to type and edit source code for .JAVA files, .HTML files, and other text files. The editor has advanced features that support text search and replacement (see Part II).

✦ **Compiler and linker:** Compile and link your source code to generate executable files that either run as stand-alone applications or as applets running in Web pages.

✦ **Java Applet Wizard:** Allows you to quickly and easily create skeleton Java source code files. You then need to add your own statements to customize the code generated by the Java Applet Wizard.

✦ **Debugger:** Allows you to set and manage breakpoints, single-step in programs, and inspect the values in attributes and variables (see Part II).

✦ **Integrated Help system:** Allows you to obtain help by searching for keywords or by pressing the F1 function key when the cursor is on a keyword in a source code window.

The Java Applet Wizard

When you install Visual J++, it adds the Java Applet Wizard to the Developer Studio. This wizard permits you to choose various options to customize the creation of the skeleton Java applet. You can then insert additional statements in the source code files to support the specific features of your applets.

Creating a Java applet

To use the Java Applet Wizard to create a Java applet, perform the following steps:

1. Choose File⇨New to create a file. The Developer Studio displays the New dialog box. Click the Projects tab.

2. Type the project name (for example, Minimal) in the Project name text box and click the OK button.

You can use the Location text box (or the browse button location to its right) to select the folder to which the new project folder will be attached.

3. Select the Java Applet Wizard item from the Projects list and click OK.

From this point forward, the Developer Studio displays five dialog boxes, which are labeled Step 1 of 5 through Step 5 of 5. Click the Next button to move to the next dialog box. Click the Back button to view the previous dialog box.

When you click the Finish button (or click the Finish button in any Step dialog box), the Developer Studio displays the New Project Information dialog box. This dialog box displays a summary of the project. When you click the OK button, the Developer Studio generates the files for the project. These files include the HTML and Java source code files as well as other files (such as DSW and DSP files) to manage the project and relate the files to each other.

Creating a basic Java application

The following example uses the Java Applet Wizard to create a
basic Java application (which shows you some of the features that
are built into the AWT library). This example shows you the power
of the AWT library that is used by the Java Applet Wizard. To use
the Java Applet Wizard, perform the following steps:

1. Choose File⇨New to create a file. The Developer Studio
   displays the New dialog box. Select the Projects page.

2. Type the project name **MinApp** in the Project name text box.
   Click the OK button.

3. Select the Java Applet Wizard item from the Projects list and
   then click OK.

4. Click the Next button in each of the first four Step dialog
   boxes and click the Finish button in the Step 5 dialog box.

5. Click the OK button in the New Project Information dialog box.
   The Java Applet Wizard generates the source code files for you.

The project MinApp contains the files MINAPP.HTML and
MINAPP.JAVA. The following is the source code for MINAPP.HTML:

```
<html>
<head>
<title>MinApp</title>
</head>
<body>
<hr>
<applet
    code=MinApp.class
    name=MinApp
    width=320
    height=240 >
</applet>
<hr>
<a href="MinApp.java">The source.</a>
</body>
</html>
```

This HTML file contains the applet tag with the parameters code,
name, width, and height. The code parameter indicates that the
browser should load and run the compiled Java class in the file
MINAPP.CLASS. The name parameter specifies that the applet
name is MinApp. The width and height parameters indicate that
the drawing area is 320 pixels wide and 240 pixels high, respectively.

The following is the source code for the MINAPP.JAVA file (I edited
the output, especially the comments, to fit this book's format —
but don't worry, the result is the same):

```
//
    ***********************************************************
    // MinApp.java:  Applet
//
//
    ***********************************************************
    import java.applet.*;
import java.awt.*;

//
    ===========================================================
    // Main Class for applet MinApp
//
//
    ===========================================================
    public class MinApp extends Applet implements
    Runnable
{
  // THREAD SUPPORT:
  //    m_MinApp is the Thread object for the applet
  //    ────────────────────────
        private Thread    m_MinApp = null;

  //    ANIMATION SUPPORT:
  //    m_Graphics     used for storing the applet's
  //    Graphics context
  //    m_Images[]     the array of Image objects
  //    for the animation
  //    m_nCurrImage   the index of the next image
  //                   to be displayed
  //    m_ImgWidth     width of each image
  //    m_ImgHeight    height of each image
  //    m_fAllLoaded   indicates whether all images
  //                   have been loaded
  //    NUM_IMAGES     number of images used in the
  //                   animation
  //────────────────────────
    private Graphics m_Graphics;
    private Image    m_Images[];
    private int      m_nCurrImage;
    private int      m_nImgWidth  = 0;
    private int      m_nImgHeight = 0;
    private boolean  m_fAllLoaded = false;
    private final int NUM_IMAGES = 18;


  // MinApp Class Constructor
  //────────────────────────
  public MinApp()
  {
    // TODO: Add constructor code here
  }

  // APPLET INFO SUPPORT:
  // The getAppletInfo() method returns a string
```

(continued)

(continued)

```java
// describing the applet's author, copyright
// date,
// or miscellaneous information.
//──────────────────────────────
public String getAppletInfo()
{
  return "Name: MinApp\r\n" +
       "Author: Namir Shammas\r\n" +
       "Created with Microsoft Visual J++ Version
 1.1";
}


// The init() method is called by the AWT when an
// applet is first loaded or reloaded.  Override
// this method to perform whatever initialization
// your applet needs, such as initializing data
// structures, loading images or fonts, creating
// frame windows, setting the layout manager, or
// adding UI components.
//──────────────────────────────
public void init()
{
      // If you use a ResourceWizard-generated
      // "control creator" class to arrange
      // controls in your applet, you may want to
      // call its CreateControls() method from
      // within this method. Remove the following
      // call to resize() before adding the call
      // to CreateControls();
      // CreateControls() does its own resizing.
      //──────────────────────────
      resize(320, 240);

      // TODO: Place additional initialization
      // code here
}

// Place additional applet cleanup code
// here.destroy()
// is called when your applet is terminating and
// being unloaded.
//──────────────────────────────
public void destroy()
{
  // TODO: Place applet cleanup code here
}

  // ANIMATION SUPPORT:
  //     Draws the next image, if all images are
  //     currently loaded
  //──────────────────────────────
private void displayImage(Graphics g)
{
  if (!m_fAllLoaded)
```

```
        return;

  // Draw Image in center of applet
  //—————————————————————————
  g.drawImage(m_Images[m_nCurrImage],
        (size().width  - m_nImgWidth)  / 2,
        (size().height - m_nImgHeight) / 2,
  null);
}

// MinApp Paint Handler
//—————————————————————————
public void paint(Graphics g)
{
  // ANIMATION SUPPORT:
  // The following code displays a status message
  // until all the images are loaded. Then it
  // calls displayImage to display the current
  // image.
  //—————————————————————————
  if (m_fAllLoaded)
  {
    Rectangle r = g.getClipRect();

    g.clearRect(r.x, r.y, r.width, r.height);
    displayImage(g);
  }
  else
    g.drawString("Loading images...", 10, 20);

  // TODO: Place additional applet Paint code
  // here
}

// The start() method is called when the page
// containing the applet first appears on the
// screen. The AppletWizard's initial
// implementation of this method starts execution
// of the applet's thread.
//—————————————————————————
public void start()
{
  if (m_MinApp == null)
  {
    m_MinApp = new Thread(this);
    m_MinApp.start();
  }
  // TODO: Place additional applet start code
  // here
}

// The stop() method is called when the page
// containing the applet is no longer on the
// screen. The AppletWizard's initial
// implementation of this method stops execution
```

(continued)

(continued)

```
// of the applet's thread.
//
  public void stop()
{
  if (m_MinApp != null)
  {
    m_MinApp.stop();
    m_MinApp = null;
  }

  // TODO: Place additional applet stop code here
}

// THREAD SUPPORT
// The run() method is called when the applet's
// thread is started. If your applet performs any
// ongoing activities without waiting for user
// input, the code for implementing that behavior
// typically goes here. For example, for an
// applet that performs animation, the run()
// method controls the display of images.
//
public void run()
{
  m_nCurrImage = 0;

  // If re-entering the page, then the images
  // have already been loaded.
  // m_fAllLoaded == TRUE.
  //
    if (!m_fAllLoaded)
  {
    repaint();
    m_Graphics = getGraphics();
    m_Images   = new Image[NUM_IMAGES];

    // Load in all the images
    //
    MediaTracker tracker = new
MediaTracker(this);
    String strImage;

    // For each image in the animation, this
    // method first constructs a string
    // containing the path to the image file;
    // then it begins loading the image into
    // the m_Images array. Note that the call
    // to getImage will return before the
    // image is completely loaded.
    //
    for (int i = 1; i <= NUM_IMAGES; i++)
    {
      // Build path to next image
      //
```

```
       strImage = "images/img00" +
          ((i < 10) ? "0" : "") + i + ".gif";
       m_Images[i-1] =
getImage(getDocumentBase(),
                                strImage);

            tracker.addImage(m_Images[i-1], 0);
    }

  // Wait until all images are fully loaded
  //——————————————————
  try
  {
    tracker.waitForAll();
    m_fAllLoaded = !tracker.isErrorAny();
  }
  catch (InterruptedException e)
  {
    // TODO: Place exception-handling code here
    // in case an InterruptedException is
    // thrown by Thread.sleep(),meaning that
    // another thread has interrupted this one
  }

  if (!m_fAllLoaded)
  {
      stop();
      m_Graphics.drawString("Error loading
images!",
                            10, 40);
      return;
  }


  // Assuming all images are same width and
  // height.
  // ——————————————————
    m_nImgWidth  = m_Images[0].getWidth(this);
    m_nImgHeight = m_Images[0].getHeight(this);
    }
repaint();

while (true)
{
  try
  {
    // Draw next image in animation
    //——————————————————
    displayImage(m_Graphics);
    m_nCurrImage++;
    if (m_nCurrImage == NUM_IMAGES)
      m_nCurrImage = 0;

    // TODO:  Add additional thread-specific
    // code here
    Thread.sleep(50);
  }
```

(continued)

(continued)

```
      catch (InterruptedException e)
      {
        // TODO: Place exception-handling code here
        // in case an InterruptedException is
        // thrown by Thread.sleep(), meaning that
        // another thread has interrupted this one
        stop();
      }
    }
  }

  // TODO: Place additional applet code here

}
```

The code in file MINAPP.JAVA declares the class MinApp as an extension to the class Applet (which runs Java applets). The class packages attributes and methods. The attributes are as follows:

+ The attribute m_Graphics helps the program display animation.

+ The attribute m_Images stores the images that are read from the GIF files.

+ The attribute m_nCurrImage is an index to the currently visible image.

+ The attributes m_nImgWidth and m_nImgHeight store the width and height of an image, respectively.

+ The attribute m_fAllLoaded is a flag that tells the program whether it loaded all of the images to proceed with the animation.

+ The attribute NUM_IMAGES stores the number of images.

+ The attribute m_MinApp,which is a Thread object, supports the animation.

The class MinApp contains the following methods:

+ The constructor MinApp()has no code.

+ The method getAppletInfo() returns the applet information.

+ The method init() is invoked once to initialize an applet after that applet is loaded into the system.

+ The method destroy() is called to tell the applet how to reclaim special resources.

+ The method paint() draws the contents of the drawing area.

+ The method start() tells the applet what to do to start running. Use this method to support multithreading.

✦ The method `stop()` tells the applet what to do to stop its execution.

✦ The method `run()` tells the applet what to do to support a thread (that is, a task).

✦ The method `displayImage()` displays an image.

Therefore, the class `MinApp` packages the preceding attributes and methods to support the animation.

The JVIEW Interpreter

When you ask the Developer Studio to execute a Java console application, it launches the JVIEW interpreter. This interpreter executes the complied code in a .CLASS file that the Visual J++ compiler created. The JVIEW interpreter runs Java programs that do not support graphical user interface. Instead, these programs are text based and accept keyboard input. This interpreter is very useful in teaching the core components of the Java language. The file for the JVIEW interpreter (JVIEW.EXE) resides in the Windows directory.

Projects

As programs get more sophisticated, they require the use and support of multiple files. The Developer Studio uses project files to store files for one or more programming projects. As a novice Visual J++ programmer, you'll typically store the files of a program project in a single project file. The Developer Studio uses the .DSP (short for Developer Studio Project) files to store projects. Project files are text files that describe the files involved in the projects. These files are typically .JAVA (Java source code) files, .HTML (Web page) files, .DSW (Developer Studio Workspace) files, and other binary files.

Here is a sample .DSP for the `Minimal` project (just to give you an idea!):

```
# Microsoft Developer Studio Project File -
    Name="Minimal" - Package Owner=<4>
# Microsoft Developer Studio Generated Build File,
    Format Version 5.00
# ** DO NOT EDIT **

# TARGTYPE "Java Virtual Machine Java Project"
    0x0809

CFG=Minimal - Java Virtual Machine Debug
```

(continued)

(continued)

```
!MESSAGE This is not a valid makefile. To build
   this project using NMAKE,
!MESSAGE use the Export Makefile command and run
!MESSAGE
!MESSAGE NMAKE /f "Minimal.mak".
!MESSAGE
!MESSAGE You can specify a configuration when
   running NMAKE
!MESSAGE by defining the macro CFG on the command
   line. For example:
!MESSAGE
!MESSAGE NMAKE /f "Minimal.mak" CFG="Minimal - Java
   Virtual Machine Debug"
!MESSAGE
!MESSAGE Possible choices for configuration are:
!MESSAGE
!MESSAGE "Minimal - Java Virtual Machine Release"
   (based on\
 "Java Virtual Machine Java Project")
!MESSAGE "Minimal - Java Virtual Machine Debug"
   (based on\
 "Java Virtual Machine Java Project")
!MESSAGE

# Begin Project
# PROP Scc_ProjName ""
# PROP Scc_LocalPath ""
JAVA=jvc.exe

!IF  "$(CFG)" == "Minimal - Java Virtual Machine
   Release"

# PROP BASE Use_MFC 0
# PROP BASE Use_Debug_Libraries 0
# PROP BASE Output_Dir ""
# PROP BASE Intermediate_Dir ""
# PROP BASE Target_Dir ""
# PROP Use_MFC 0
# PROP Use_Debug_Libraries 0
# PROP Output_Dir ""
# PROP Intermediate_Dir ""
# PROP Target_Dir ""
# ADD BASE JAVA /O
# ADD JAVA /O

!ELSEIF  "$(CFG)" == "Minimal - Java Virtual
   Machine Debug"

# PROP BASE Use_MFC 0
# PROP BASE Use_Debug_Libraries 1
# PROP BASE Output_Dir ""
# PROP BASE Intermediate_Dir ""
# PROP BASE Target_Dir ""
# PROP Use_MFC 0
# PROP Use_Debug_Libraries 1
```

```
# PROP Output_Dir ""
# PROP Intermediate_Dir ""
# PROP Target_Dir ""
# ADD BASE JAVA /g
# ADD JAVA /g

!ENDIF

# Begin Target

# Name "Minimal - Java Virtual Machine Release"
# Name "Minimal - Java Virtual Machine Debug"
# Begin Group "Source Files"

# PROP Default_Filter "java;html"
# Begin Source File

SOURCE=.\Minimal.html
# End Source File
# Begin Source File

SOURCE=.\Minimal.java
# End Source File
# End Group
# Begin Group "Resource Files"

# PROP Default_Filter
    "ico;cur;bmp;dlg;rc2;rct;bin;cnt;rtf;gif;jpg;jpeg;jpe"
# Begin Source File

SOURCE=.\images\img0001.gif
# End Source File
# Begin Source File

SOURCE=.\images\img0002.gif
# End Source File
# Begin Source File

SOURCE=.\images\img0003.gif
# End Source File
# Begin Source File

SOURCE=.\images\img0004.gif
# End Source File
# Begin Source File

SOURCE=.\images\img0005.gif
# End Source File
# Begin Source File

SOURCE=.\images\img0006.gif
# End Source File
# Begin Source File

SOURCE=.\images\img0007.gif
```

(continued)

(continued)

```
# End Source File
# Begin Source File

SOURCE=.\images\img0008.gif
# End Source File
# Begin Source File

SOURCE=.\images\img0009.gif
# End Source File
# Begin Source File

SOURCE=.\images\img0010.gif
# End Source File
# Begin Source File

SOURCE=.\images\img0011.gif
# End Source File
# Begin Source File

SOURCE=.\images\img0012.gif
# End Source File
# Begin Source File

SOURCE=.\images\img0013.gif
# End Source File
# Begin Source File

SOURCE=.\images\img0014.gif
# End Source File
# Begin Source File

SOURCE=.\images\img0015.gif
# End Source File
# Begin Source File

SOURCE=.\images\img0016.gif
# End Source File
# Begin Source File

SOURCE=.\images\img0017.gif
# End Source File
# Begin Source File

SOURCE=.\images\img0018.gif
# End Source File
# End Group
# End Target
# End Project
```

Adding files to a project

The Developer Studio allows you to add files to a project. This
feature is very useful, especially when you create a Java project

without using the Java Applet Wizard. In this case, you need to create the project's source code files separately and then insert them into the project. (See "Text Files," later in this part.)

To insert a file in the current project, follow these steps:

✦ Choose Project⬩Add to Project⬩Files. This command opens the Insert Files into Project dialog box. This dialog box is basically a common Open dialog box.

✦ Select the file type in the Files of type list box. This list box contains the list of all types of files that the Developer Studio is aware of, based on the Developer Studio components installed.

✦ Select the file that you want to insert from the list of files by clicking that file.

✦ Click the OK button to close the dialog box and insert the selected file. You may click the Cancel button to abort the file insertion.

Compiling a project

You can compile a Java source code file by choosing Build⬩Compile. The Developer Studio customizes the Compile command to include the name of the active file. For example, if the active file is UseText.java, the menu displays the command Compile UseText.java.

The compiler displays the status of the compilation in the Output window. This window displays a list of errors and warnings generated by the compiler. If there are errors or warnings, the Output window lists the location of the offending lines and includes an explanation for the error or warning. To jump to the offending line in the source code, click the reference to that line in the Output window.

Creating a Java project

The Developer Studio allows you to create a Java project by using the following steps:

1. Choose File⬩New. The Developer Studio displays the New dialog box. This dialog box has several tabs: Files, Projects, Workspaces, and Other Documents.

2. Click the Projects tab to select a list of project types that are available in the Developer Studio. This list varies depending on the compilers that you have installed. The next figure shows the list (on my computer) that includes projects for Visual J++ and Visual C++.

3. Select either the Java Applet Wizard or the Java Project from the list of projects.

4. Optionally, select a new folder to become the parent folder of your new project by clicking the ellipsis button that is next to the Location text box. This button displays a dialog box that allows you to select a new parent folder to which your project's folder is attached. Close the dialog box when you're finished selecting a new parent folder.

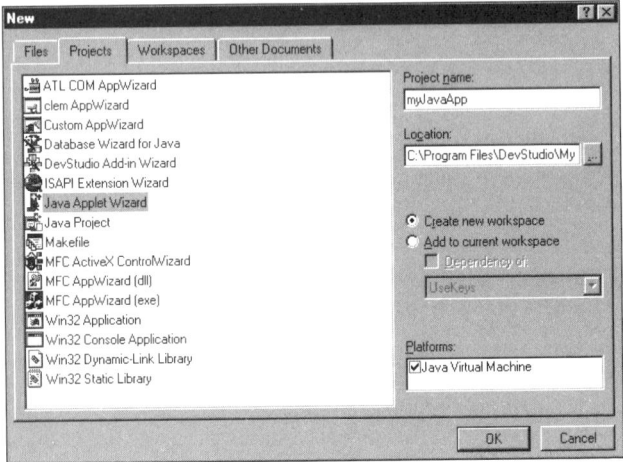

5. Enter the project name in the Project name text box.

6. Click the OK button. If you elect to use the Java Applet Wizard, the wizard displays the dialog boxes that fine-tune creating the new Java project. An earlier section, "The Java Applet Wizard: Creating Applets," describes the steps that are involved in using the wizard.

Running a project

The Developer Studio simplifies the process of compiling, linking, and running programs. As a novice Java programmer, you have the following options:

✦ Press Ctrl+F5 to run the program at the usual speed, whether or not the source code has breakpoints. You can also choose Build⇨Execute (project name) to perform the same task.

✦ Press F5 to run the program and stop at any breakpoint that it encounters. If there are no breakpoints, pressing F5 has the same effect as pressing Ctrl+F5.

In either case, if the compiler encounters errors, it does not run the program. Instead, the compiler displays errors and warning messages in the output window.

Saving a project

To save a project, the Developer Studio offers the Save Workspace command in the File menu. This command stores all of the project's files that need updating. To open a project, select File⇨Open Workspace. This command opens a dialog box that allows you to select a project to open. You can also use the Recent Workspace command to obtain a list of the most recently opened projects and to open one of these projects.

You can also click the Go button (which looks a document with a down arrow next to it) to perform the same task.

Project Workspace

Workspaces are closely related to projects. When you create a new project, the Developer Studio creates a .DSW workspace file to store information at the workspace level. This information in-cludes what files are in the workspace, the size and configuration of the various windows, breakpoints, selected text, and so on. When you save the project's file, you really save the workspace in a file. From then on, you open the workspace file, which also opens the associated files, including the .DSP project file, .JAVA file, .HTML file, and any other file. Moreover, you restore the windows configuration, breakpoints, selected text, and so on.

A Simple Visual J++ Program

In this section, I show you a simple Java program that presents the main and typical program components. The following is the traditional Hello World! program that you see in virtually every programming-language book:

```
class HiThere {
   /*
      Declare the method main which is the
      starting point for any Java applet
   */
   public static void main (String args[]) {
      // display the greeting message to
      // the standard output
      System.out.println("Hello World!");
   }
}
```

This code declares the class `HiThere`, which contains the method `main()`. This method (a part of the program that does something) is the starting point for executing a Java *applet* (a fancy word for small application). The code shows that Java supports two types of comments. The first type uses the characters `/*` and `*/` and allows you to place comments on one or more lines. Then, the second type of comment uses the `//` characters to support comments that span to the end of the same line. The method `main` displays the greeting message using the method `System.out.println()` to display the quoted text on the standard output.

Starting Visual J++

Because Visual J++ is integrated in the Developer Studio, you must run the latter to access Visual J++. To run the Developer Studio, perform the following steps:

1. Click the Start button in the Windows 95 toolbar.

2. Choose Programs⇨Microsoft Visual C++⇨Microsoft Developer Studio. You now have access to Visual J++.

Text Files

When using Visual J++, you type text in .JAVA files that represents Java source code. You also type Web page source code in .HTML files. These kinds of text files represent your instructions to the computer. However, because the computer cannot understand these instructions, Visual J++ uses support programs such as the compiler, linker, and Internet Explorer to digest and convert your text into low-level instructions that can be executed by your machine. The Developer Studio uses project files to determine how the various kinds of text files work together in creating a program. When you want to modify your program, you load and then edit the text files that contain the source code you wish to change. Then you invoke the same steps you used to create your first program version to generate a new version.

Adding text files to a project

See the section on "Projects," earlier in this part.

Creating a text file

The Developer Studio allows you to create a text file by following these steps:

1. Choose File⇨New. The Developer Studio displays the New dialog box. This dialog box has several tabs: Files, Projects, Workspaces, and Other Documents.

2. Click the Files tab to select a list of file types that are available in the Developer Studio. This list varies depending on what compilers you have installed. The next figure shows the list (on my computer) that includes projects for Visual J++ and Visual C++.

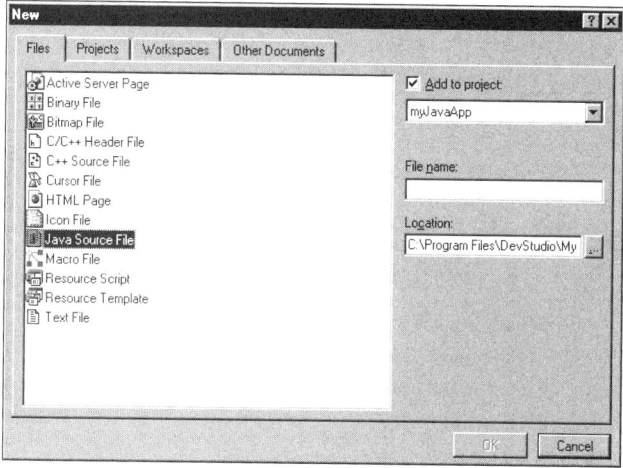

3. Select Java Source File or HTML Page. (These are the file types that most Visual J++ programmers use.)

4. To include this file in the current project, make sure that the Add to Project check box is checked.

5. Click the OK button. The Developer Studio closes the dialog box and displays the window for the new text file. Type text in the file that you just created. Save the text in your new file by clicking the Save button.

Saving a text file

The Developer Studio allows you to save the active file (or a file that you select from the FileView pane) by using the Save or Save As commands in the File menu. The Developer Studio is smart enough to know whether the file that you selected has been updated and therefore needs to be saved. If the file has not been updated, the Developer Studio knows that it does not need to be saved. In this case, the Developer Studio disables the Save command.

When you save a file for the first time, use the Save As command. This command opens the Save As dialog box (which is a dialog box that is common to Windows 95) to allow you to save the file using the name of your choice. The Developer Studio opens the same dialog box when you select the Save command with a new file. Use the Save command to update the contents of a file after you have edited these contents in its active window.

Workspace Window

The Workspace window contains several panes:

+ **ClassView:** To view class information.

+ **FileView:** To view project file information.

+ **InfoView:** To view help information.

To view the Workspace window (it's usually visible), choose View⇨Workspace.

The ClassView Pane

The ClassView pane shows the outline of the classes and their methods and attributes. You can expand or contract that outline by clicking the plus or minus buttons that are located to the left of each outline item.

If you click an attribute or method with the left mouse button, the Developer Studio displays the source code file (if it's not already visible) and then moves the cursor to the declaration of the attribute or method that you clicked. You also can click the right mouse button to display a pop-up menu.

The FileView Pane

You can view the FileView pane in the Workspace window of the Developer Studio by clicking the FileView tab. The FileView pane displays an outline that shows the current projects, their source files, and their resource files. You can expand or contract that outline by clicking the plus or minus buttons that are located to the left of each outline item. The following figure shows a sample FileView pane for a Java project that I created with the Java Applet Wizard. When you double-click a file, the Developer Studio displays that file in a window to the right of the FileView pane. If you double-click a GIF graphics file, for example, the Developer Studio displays that graphics file and includes color and toolbox palettes.

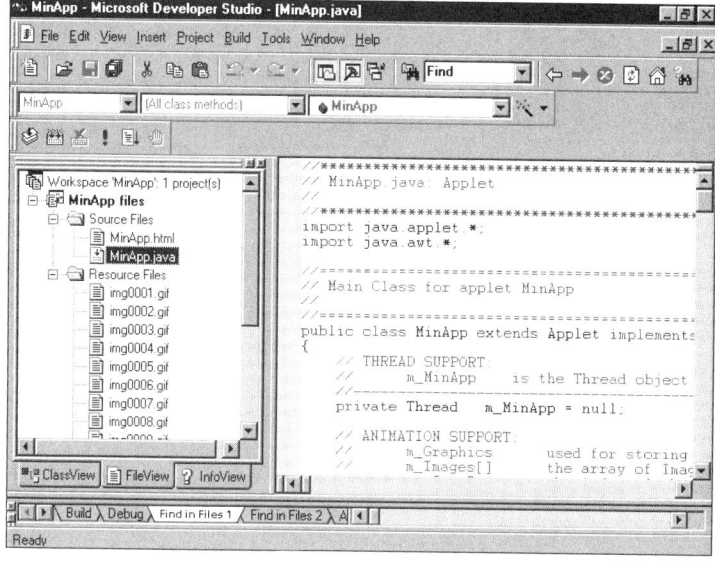

The InfoView Pane

You can view the InfoView pane in the Workspace window of the Developer Studio by clicking the InfoView tab. The InfoView pane displays an outline that shows the online help files. (Don't confuse this term with being online using a modem.) You can expand or contract that outline by clicking the plus or minus buttons that are located to the left of each outline item. The following figure shows a sample InfoView pane.

The outline contains a hierarchy of volumes, books, chapters, and documents. When you click a document, the Developer Studio displays that document in a window that is located on the right side of the InfoView pane. The online documentation typically includes hypertext links that allow you to jump to other locations in the same document or to other documents.

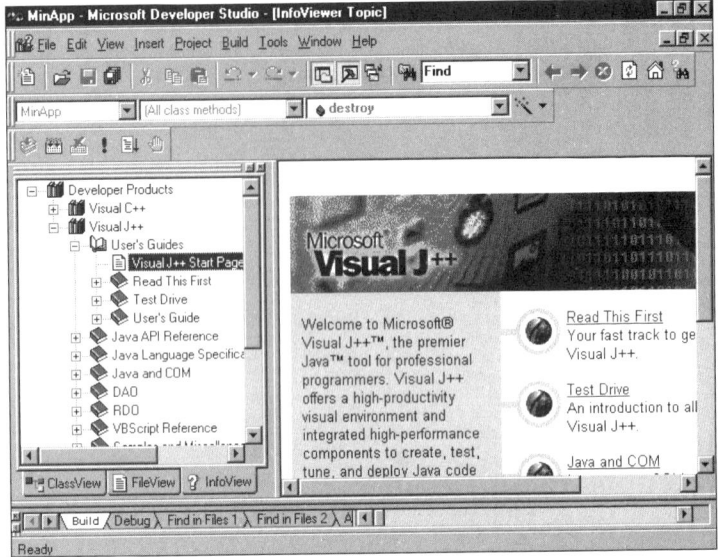

## Part II

Editing and Debugging

This part looks at two aspects of programming with Visual J++ : editing and debugging. The material in this part covers two important aspects of editing files, namely, finding and replacing text. In addition, this part refreshes your skills in debugging programs. This process include setting breakpoints to pause the program execution, single-stepping in program statements, and inspecting the values in variables and attributes.

In this part

✔ **Working with breakpoints**

✔ **Debugging programs**

✔ **Finding text**

✔ **Replacing text**

✔ **Stepping in a program**

✔ **Watching variables**

Breakpoints

A *breakpoint* allows you to stop the program execution at a specific statement to examine the value of one or more attributes and/or variables (see "Variables," later in this part). There are two kinds of breakpoints: unconditional and conditional.

✦ **Unconditional breakpoint:** Causes the program to stop at the statement where you place that breakpoint. The program stops at that point every time it encounters that breakpoint.

✦ **Conditional breakpoint:** Causes the program to stop at the statement where you place that breakpoint when a condition associated with that breakpoint is true.

Clearing breakpoints

To clear a breakpoint, perform the following steps:

1. Open the source code file in which you have inserted one or more breakpoints.

2. Locate the statement that has a breakpoint. (Each statement that has a breakpoint has a red dot to its left.) You may need to scroll up or down to locate the statement.

3. Click the Insert/Remove Breakpoint toolbar button or press F9. The Developer Studio removes the red dot and clears the breakpoint.

To remove all the breakpoints in a file, perform the following steps:

1. Choose Edit⬩Breakpoints. The Developer Studio displays the Breakpoints dialog box.

2. Click the Remove All button to remove all breakpoints.

Saving files with breakpoints

You can save the breakpoints that you set in a file by choosing File⬩Save Workspace. The next time that you load the same project, the source code window displays the breakpoints that you had set up.

Setting conditional breakpoints

To set a conditional breakpoint in source code, first set an unconditional breakpoint (see the section "Setting Uncondtional breakpoints") and then perform the following steps:

1. Choose Edit➪Breakpoints. The Developer Studio displays the Breakpoints dialog box.

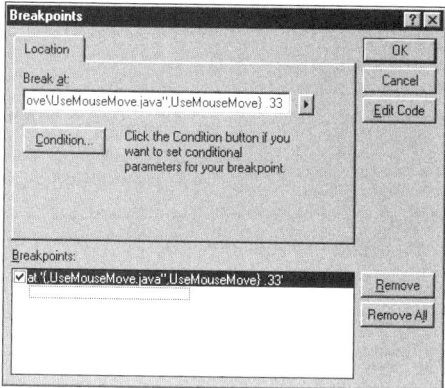

2. From the list of breakpoints, click the breakpoint you want.

3. Click the Condition button. The Developer Studio displays the Breakpoint Condition dialog box.

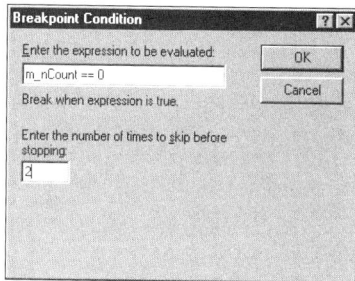

4. If you want the program to stop when a particular expression is true, enter the expression that you want evaluated in the first text box. Or, in the second text box, enter the number of times to skip the breakpoint before the program stops. You also may enter a combination of both. Click OK when you're done.

5. Click the OK button to close the Breakpoint Condition dialog box.

6. Repeat Steps 2 and 5 for other breakpoints.

7. Click the OK button to close the Breakpoints dialog box.

Setting unconditional breakpoints

To set an unconditional breakpoint, perform the following steps:

1. Open the source code file in which you want to insert one or more breakpoints.

2. Locate the statement at which you want to set the breakpoint. You may need to scroll the source code up or down to locate that statement.

3. Click the Insert/Remove Breakpoint toolbar button (it looks like an upright hand) or press F9. The Developer Studio places a breakpoint at that statement and displays a red dot to the left of the statement that contains the breakpoint.

Debugging Programs

When a program doesn't work as you intended, examine the source code to detect logical or runtime errors. Logical errors occur when the program works fine, but is not doing what you want it to do. Runtime errors occur when the program attempts to perform an illegal task. If this examination works, you have solved your problem. If not, your next move is to debug the program. *Debugging* a program involves running the program in a special mode that allows you to stop it at certain points, examine the values in the variables and attributes, and run the program one step at a time (this is called *tracing* the execution of a program). This technique allows you to detect erroneous values in variables and attributes, determine that the program is not executing statements that you think it should, or both.

Debugging a program includes the following tasks:

+ **Setting breakpoints**. See the section "Breakpoints," earlier in this part.

+ **Setting Watch variables.** See the section "Watching Variables," later in this part.

+ **Single-stepping in a program when the program stops at a breakpoint.** See the section "Stepping in a Program," later in this part.

The following is a simple test program (named USEDEBUG.JAVA) that puts the preceding tasks to work. To find out how to create this test program, see "The Java Applet Wizard" in Part I. The test program adds the from 1 and 10 (during the initialization of the program) and displays that sum in the drawing area.

```
import java.applet.*
import java.awt.*;

public class UseDebug extends Applet
{
    protected String m_Message;

    public String getAppletInfo()
    {
        return "";
    }

    public void init()
    {
        double fSum = 0;

        resize(320, 240);
        for (int i = 1; i < 11; i++)
            fSum += (double)i;
        m_Message = "Sum of 1 to 10 = " + fSum;
    }

    public void paint(Graphics g)
    {
        g.drawString(m_Message, 10, 20);
    }
}
```

This code declares the attribute and methods for the class
UseDebug. The class declares the String-type attribute
m_Message, which stores the text that appears in the drawing area.

The method init() initializes the form by using a for loop to
add the numbers from 1 to 10 in the local double-type variable
fSum. The method then stores a message with the value of
variable fSum in the attribute m_Message.

The method paint displays the text in the attribute m_Message
by sending the message drawString() to Graphics object g. The
arguments for this message are the attribute m_Message and the
coordinates 10 and 20.

You can trace the program's for loop (which uses the control
variable *i*) in the method init() to watch the progress in updating the values in the variable fSum. Perform the following tasks:

1. Open the USEDEBUG.JAVA file (if it is not already open).

2. Move the cursor to the resize() statement in the method
init().

3. Press F9 to insert an unconditional breakpoint. (See the section
"Setting unconditional breakpoints," earlier in this part.)

4. Press F5 to start running the program in debug mode. In debug mode, the program stops at breakpoints and allows you to single step program statements and inspect the values in variables. If you're running this program for the first time, the Developer Studio displays a message asking you to create the program's executable files. Click the Yes button. The Developer Studio displays the HTML file using Microsoft Internet Explorer and then switches back to the Studio's window to show the source code in debug mode.

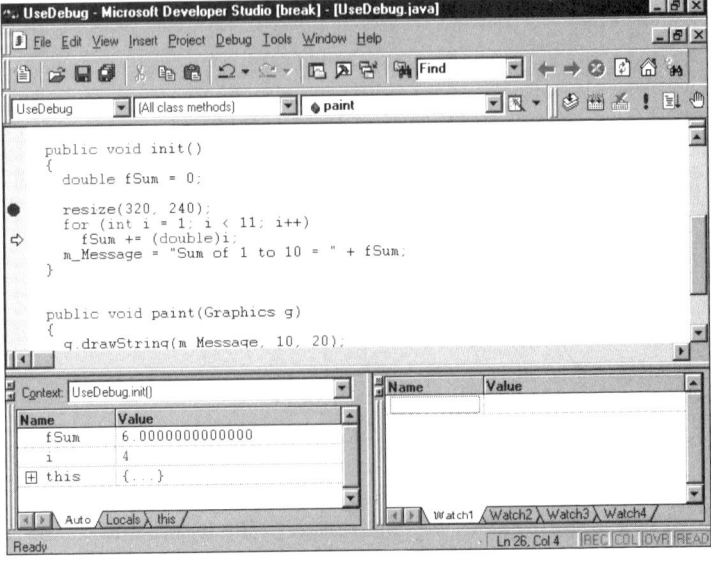

5. To trace the execution of the loop, press F10 and watch the values of the variables *i* and fSum change, as shown in the lower-left window. The following table displays the values for the variables *i* and fSum as you single-step the loop's statement using the F10 key.

6. When the loop ends, press Ctrl+F5 to resume the program's execution. The program then displays the HTML page showing the text "The sum of 1 to 10 is 55".

Loop Iteration No.	Value in Variable i	Value in Variable fSum
Initial	1	0
1	1	1
2	2	3
3	3	6

Loop Iteration No.	Value in Variable i	Value in Variable fSum
4	4	10
5	5	15
6	6	21
7	7	28
8	8	36
9	9	45
10	10	55

Finding Text

The Developer Studio supports simple and advanced text searches. The simple text search uses the Find command in the Edit menu. The advanced text search uses the Find in Files command in the Edit menu.

The Find command

The Find command allows you to locate text in files that are currently opened. This command displays the Find dialog box. This dialog box contains the following components:

◆ **The Find what text box:** Enter the text that you want to locate in this box. You can click the down arrow that is associated with the text box to view the text for previous searches.

◆ **The right-arrow button:** This button, located next to the Find what text box, displays a pop-up menu that contains the items used to search for text patterns (used in conjunction with the regular expression type of search).

◆ **The Match whole word only check box:** When you check this box, the search looks for a whole word that matches the text in the Find what text box. Otherwise, the search locates any occurrence of the search text.

◆ **The Match case check box:** When you check this box, the Developer Studio conducts a case-sensitive search. Otherwise, the search is case insensitive.

◆ **The Regular expression check box:** When you check this box, the Developer Studio uses the search text as a text pattern and not verbatim text — this feature is an advanced one. Therefore, if you're a new Visual J++ user, I suggest that you avoid checking this box.

✦ **Search all open documents check box:** When you check this box, the Developer Studio searches all the opened files. Otherwise, the Developer Studio limits its search to the text in the active window.

✦ **The Direction buttons, namely, Up and Down:** These buttons allow you to specify the search direction. By default, the search is downward.

✦ **The Find button:** This button starts the search for the next matching text.

✦ **The Find Next button:** This button (which appears after you press the Find button and replaces that button) searches for the next matching text.

✦ **The Mark All button:** This button marks all the matching text by displaying a rounded rectangle to the left of every line that contains the matching text.

✦ **The Cancel button:** This button allows you to cancel searching for text or stop searching for more text.

The Find in Files command

The Find in Files command allows you to locate text in multiple text files that are opened. This command displays the Find in Files dialog box. This dialog box contains the following components:

✦ **The Find what text box:** Enter the text that you want to locate in this box. You can click the down arrow that is associated with the text box to view the text for previous searches.

✦ **The right-arrow button:** This button, located next to the Find what text box, displays a pop-up menu that contains items that are used to search for text patterns (used in conjunction with the regular expression type of search).

✦ **The In files/file types text box:** Enter the wildcard for the files that you want to search. For example, the wildcard *.java searches in all files with a JAVA suffix. You can click the down arrow that is associated with the text box to view the previous filename wildcards that you entered.

✦ **The In folder text box:** Enter the name of the folder that you want to search. You can click the down arrow that is associated with the text box to view the names of previously selected folders. You can also click the ellipsis button located to the right of the text box. This button opens a dialog box that allows you to select a target folder.

✦ **The Match whole word only check box:** When you check this box, the search looks for a whole word that matches the text

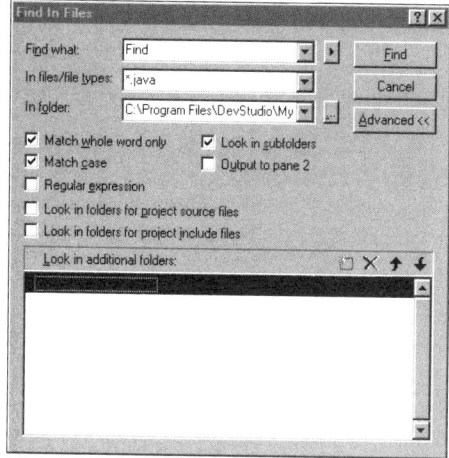

in the Find what text box. Otherwise, the search locates any occurrence of the search text.

◆ **The Match _c_ase check box:** When you check this box, the Developer Studio conducts a case-sensitive search. Otherwise, the search is case insensitive.

◆ **The Regular _e_xpression check box:** When you check this box, the Developer Studio uses the search text (which should contain special regular expression commands) as a text pattern and not verbatim text.

◆ **The Look in _s_ubfolders check box:** When you check this box, the Developer Studio searches in the *parent* folder that you specify in the In folder text box and all folders that are nested in that folder.

◆ **The O_u_tput to pane 2 check box:** When you check this box, the Developer Studio displays the output to the Find in Files pane 2.

◆ **The Look in folders for _p_roject source files check box:** When you check this box, the Developer Studio searches for text in the project's source code files.

◆ **The Look in folders for project _i_nclude files check box:** When you check this box, the Developer Studio searches for text in the project's include files. These are the files that appear in C++ #include directives. Therefore, this check box does not work for Visual J++ source code files.

◆ **The _L_ook in additional folders list box:** You can add the names of additional folders in this list box. The dialog box shows four buttons near the list box to add, remove, and move up and move down the names of folders.

✦ **The Find button:** This button starts searching for the next matching text.

✦ **The Cancel button:** This button allows you to cancel searching for text or stop searching for more text.

✦ **The Advanced button:** This button toggles the visibility of the components below the Regular expression check box.

Replacing Text

The Replace command allows you to locate and replace text in the active window. This command displays the Replace dialog box. This dialog box contains the following components:

✦ **The Find what text box:** Enter the search text in this box. You can click the down arrow that is associated with the text box to view any previous search text.

✦ **The Replace with text box:** Enter the replacement text in this box. You can click the down arrow that is associated with this text box to view any previous replacement text.

✦ **The right-arrow buttons:** These buttons, located next to the two text boxes, display pop-up menus that contain items that are used to search and replace text patterns (used in conjunction with the regular expression type of search).

✦ **The Match whole word only check box:** When you check this box, the search looks for a whole word that matches the text in the Find what text box. Otherwise, the search locates any occurrence of the search text.

✦ **The Match case check box:** When you check this box, the Developer Studio conducts a case-sensitive search. Otherwise, the search is case insensitive.

✦ **The Regular expression check box:** When you check this box, the Developer Studio uses the search text as a text pattern and not verbatim text. This feature is an advanced one. Therefore, if you're a new Visual J++ user, I suggest that you avoid checking this box.

✦ **The Replace in buttons:** The Selection and Whole file buttons allow you to replace text in the selection or in the entire file. When no selected text is in the active window, the Developer Studio disables the Selection button.

✦ **The Find Next button:** This button starts the search for the next matching text.

✦ **The Replace button:** This button replaces the current text match only.

✦ **The Replace All button:** This button replaces the matched text throughout the scope defined by the check boxes and buttons in the dialog box.

✦ **The Cancel button:** This button allows you to cancel searching for text or stop searching for more text.

Stepping in a Program

When a program stops at a breakpoint (see the section "Breakpoints," earlier in this part), you can single-step through its statements and/or the statements of the methods that are called by that program. During break mode, the Developer Studio displays the Debug menu, which has the following relevant commands:

✦ **Step Into:** Allows you to trace the call to a method that was called by the current method. You can then single-step through the statements of the called method.

✦ **Step Over:** Allows you to execute all the methods that are called by the current statement, in normal speed. Use this command to skip tracing a call to a method when you know (or think you know) that the called method works properly.

✦ **Step Out:** Allows you to execute the program out of a method call and then stops on the instruction immediately following the call to that method. Use this command to end executing the call to the current method after you have decided that the method works properly.

✦ **Run to Cursor:** Causes the program to run in normal speed until it reaches the statement with the cursor. This command emulates setting a temporary breakpoint that automatically clears when the program stops.

Watching Variables

Debugging involves examining the flow-statement execution as well as viewing the values in the variables and attributes. The Developer Studio offers you two kinds of windows to watch variables and attributes.

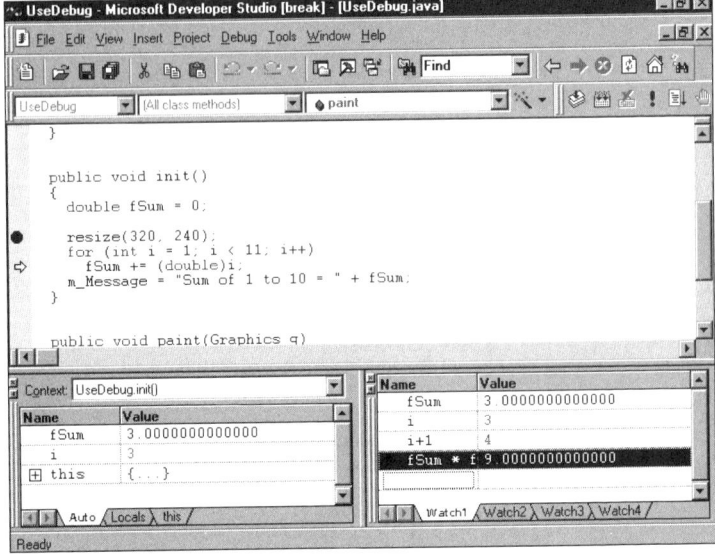

♦ The lower-left window shows the names and values of attributes and variables that are in the scope of the current method. The window has three tabs: Auto (for automatically watching variables), Locals (to view local variables), and this (to view the attributes of the current class).

♦ The lower-right window shows the names and values for variables that you enter. You also can enter expressions that include the names of variables and attributes. To enter a new variable, click an empty Name cell. To edit an existing Name cell, click that cell. This window has several tabs, allowing you to group watched variables depending on their context (that is, which method you are single-stepping through).

## Part III

Constants and Variables

This part covers the basic aspect fo Java that allows you to work with information. I cover the and predefined data types in Java and show you how to declare and use constants, variables, and arrays — programming components that allow you to store information in them. Some components, like arrays and variables, permit you to update the data they store. By contrast, constants maintain the values that you associate with them.

In this part

✔ Working with arrays

✔ Casting values

✔ Using constants

✔ Using predefined data types

✔ Working with variables

✔ Naming rules in Java

Arrays

The interesting part about arrays in Java is that you do not specify the number of elements when you declare an array.

Accessing simple arrays

Java allows you to access an array element using the name of the array and an index, which are placed in brackets. As with C and C++, the index of the first array element is 0.

The general syntax for accessing the element of a simple array is

```
arrayName[index]
```

The preceding syntax shows that you need to state the name of the array and use an index value (either a literal integer, a constant, or a variable) enclosed in square brackets.

The following are several examples of working with the simple arrays:

```
SumsArray[1] = SumsArray[0] + 12;
CharsArray[0] = 'e';
FriendsNames[2] = "Marcia";
Flags[99] = true;
MonthlyPriceArray[4] = 1.2 * MonthlyPriceArray[3];
```

The examples are explained as follows:

+ The first example takes the value in the first element (at index 0) of array SumsArray, adds 12 to it, and stores the result in the second element (at index 1) of the array SumsArray.

+ The second example assigns the character *e* to the first element (at index 0) of the array CharsArray.

+ The third example stores the student friend *Marcia* in the third array element (at index 2) of the array FriendNames.

+ The fourth example stores the logical value true in the 100th element (at index 99) of the array Flags.

+ The last example takes April's price (the fourth month stored in the fourth element of array MonthlyPriceArray), multiplies it by 1.2, and stores the result in May's price (the fifth month stored in the fifth element of the array MonthlyPriceArray).

Declaring simple arrays

Java offers two versions of the general syntax for declaring an array. The first version is as follows:

```
dataType arrayName[];
```

This version states the data type of the array elements and the name of the array and then places a pair of empty brackets after that name. The second version is as follows:

```
dataType[] arrayName;
```

This version differs from the first one in that the empty brackets appear immediately after the data type of the array elements.

Java deals with arrays somewhat differently than other languages, such as C and C++. First, Java supports dynamic arrays only. Second, Java treats arrays as objects, requiring you to use the operator `new` to create the memory space for the array elements.

The following are a few examples of declaring arrays:

```
int SumsArray[];
char CharsArray[];
String FriendsNames[];
boolean[] Flags;
double[] MonthlyPriceArray;
```

The examples are explained as follows:

◆ The first example declares the `int`-type array `SumsArray`. Therefore, the elements of this array store integers.

◆ The second example declares the `char`-type array `CharsArray`. In this case, the elements of this array store characters.

◆ The third example declares the `String`-type array `FriendsNames`. Therefore, the elements of this array store strings.

◆ The fourth example declares the `boolean`-type array `Flags`. In this case, the elements of this array store logical values.

◆ The last example declares the `double`-type array `MonthlyPriceArray`. Therefore, the elements of this array store floating-point numbers.

Note that the first three arrays use the first syntax version. The remaining array declarations use the second syntax version. A good rule of thumb is to use the version that you're comfortable with and stay with that version to make your code consistent.

Using the operator new

After you declare an array, you must specify the number of elements in that array before you can access these elements. Java offers the operator `new` to dynamically allocate the space for the array.

The general syntax for using the operator `new` to dynamically set the size of an array is as follows:

```
arrayName = new dataType[numberOfElements];
```

The following are some examples of declaring and allocating space for the arrays in two steps:

```
int CounterArray[];
CounterArray = new int[10];

char lettersArray[];
lettersArray = new char[MAX_CHARS + 1];

String StudentNames[];
StudentNames = new String[CLASS_SIZE];

boolean[] Flags;
Flags = new boolean[100];

double[] MonthlyPriceArray;
MonthlyPriceArray = new double[12];
```

The examples are explained as follows:

+ The first example declares the `int`-type array `CounterArray` and allocates 10 elements for that array.

+ The second example declares the `char`-type array `lettersArray` and allocates `MAX_CHARS + 1` elements to that array (assuming that the constant `MAX_CHAR` is already defined).

+ The third example declares the `String`-type array `StudentNames` and allocates `CLASS_SIZE` elements to that array (assuming that the constant `CLASS_SIZE` is already defined).

+ The fourth example declares the `boolean`-type array `Flags` and allocates 100 elements.

+ The last example declares the `double`-type array `MonthlyPriceArray` and allocates 12 elements to that array.

Java allows you to declare an array and specify the number of its elements in a single statement.

The general syntax (which also has two versions) for declaring an array and allocating its elements is as follows:

```
dataType arrayName[] = new
    dataType[numberOfElements];
dataType[] arrayName = new
    dataType[numberOfElements];
```

These examples take advantage of the single-statement declaration and allocation feature. The following are several examples of declaring and allocating space for arrays in one step:

```
int CounterArray[] = new int[10];
char lettersArray[] = new char[MAX_CHARS + 1];
String StudentNames[] = new String[CLASS_SIZE];
boolean[] Flags = new boolean[100];
double[] MonthlyPriceArray = new double[12];
```

The preceding examples have the same overall effect as the previous set of examples, except that the declaration and allocation of each array occur in the same statement.

Java allows you to declare an array, allocate its elements, and initialize the array in a single statement. The key feature here is that the number of initializing values (which are located in a comma-delimited list) also specifies the number of array elements.

The general syntax for declaring arrays this way is as follows:

```
dataType arrayName[] = { value1, value2, …, valueN
        };
```

The following are some examples of declaring, allocating, and initializing arrays:

```
int CounterArray[] = { 0, 0, 0 };
char lettersArray[] = { 'A', 'U', 'I', 'O', 'E' };
String StudentNames[] = { "Joey", "Logan" ,
        "George" };
boolean[] Flags = { false, false, false, false,
        false };
double[] MonthlyPriceArray = { 12.2, 13.0, 12.5,
                               13.1, 13.4, 12.9,
                               13.2, 13.4, 12.8,
                               13.1, 13.4, 12.9 };
```

The examples are explained as follows:

+ The first example declares the int-type array CounterArray and allocates three elements for that array. All three elements store the value 0.

+ The second example declares the char-type array lettersArray and allocates five elements to that array. These elements store the uppercase vowels.

+ The third example declares the String-type array StudentNames and allocates three elements to that array. The array stores the arbitrary names of students.

+ The fourth example declares the boolean-type array Flags and allocates five elements. All of the elements in the array store false.

✦ The last example declares the `double`-type array `MonthlyPriceArray` and allocates memory for 12 elements to that array. The array stores monthly prices.

Casting Values

Most popular programming-language compilers (such as Pascal, BASIC, FORTRAN, C, and C++) perform automatic data type conversions, especially in mathematical and Boolean expressions. Often, the compiler promotes an integer type into a floating-point type; Java is no exception. Moreover, Java supports the casting feature, which allows you to explicitly convert a value from one data type to another.

The general syntax for casting is as follows:

```
(newType)expression
```

The following are examples of using the casting feature:

```
char cLetter = 'A';
int nASCII = (int)cLetter;
long lASCII = (long)cLetter;
```

This code declares and initializes the `char`-type variable `cLetter`. The code also declares the `int`-type variable `nASCII` and initializes it using the `int` cast of the variable `cLetter`. In addition, the code declares the `long`-type variable `lASCII` and initializes it using the long cast of the variable `cLetter`.

Constants

A *constant,* as the name suggests, refers to a value that remains unchanged. Constants such as the number 10 or the letter *A* are *literal constants* — they represent a fixed piece of information. Java allows you to associate literal constants with names. Programmers call them *named constants.* Using names allows you to better describe a constant and makes your source code easier to read and maintain. Because you select the names for these constants, you need to declare them to tell the compiler about them. In addition, you must tell the compiler what data type and value you're associating with the constant.

Constants maintain the same values throughout the program execution. Except when you declare the constant, you can never place that constant on the left of the assignment operator (the = sign) or make it receive input data of any kind. Typically, constants appear on the left side of assignment statements and in output statements. You can use constants in any kind of statement as long as these constants are read-only data.

The following is an example:

```
final int ONE = 1;
final TWO = ONE + ONE;
```

This example declares the constants ONE and TWO. The example declares the constant ONE and assigns the integer 1 to it. By contrast, the example declares the constant TWO and assigns the value of the expression ONE + ONE to it. The second declaration shows the constant ONE on the right side of the = sign.

The general syntax for declaring a constant in Java is as follows:

```
final dataType constantName = initialValue;
```

This general syntax indicates that the declaration of a constant includes the following parts:

✦ The key word *final*, which tells the Java compiler that you're declaring a constant

✦ The data type that is associated with the constant

✦ The name of the constant

✦ The value that is associated with the constant

You can only declare constants as fixed-value attributes of a class. In other words, Java doesn't allow you to declare constants inside the methods of a class.

The following are some examples of declaring constants:

```
final int MAX_FILES = 10;
final double CRITICAL_VOLUME = 10.34;
final char PROMPT = '>';
final String MY_NAME = "Namir Shammas";
```

The examples are explained as follows:

✦ The first example declares the int-type constant MAX_FILES and assigns the value of 10 to that constant.

✦ The second example declares the double-type constant CRITICAL_VOLUME and assigns the value 10.34 to that constant.

✦ The third example declares the char-type constant PROMPT and assigns the character > to that constant.

✦ The last example declares the String-type constant MY_NAME and assigns my name to that constant.

Predefined Data Types

Java offers basic predefined data types that allow you to work with numbers (both integers and floating-point numbers) and characters. The following table shows you the predefined data types. This table includes the names of the data types, their range of values, and some examples. You use these data types in classes and as parameters of methods.

Data Type	Comment	Range	Examples
boolean	Logical	True and false	true, false
byte	8-bit integer	−128 to 127	0, 23, −56
short	16-bit integer	−32768 to 32767	1000, −2222, 0
int	32-bit integer	−2147483648 to 2147483647	65535, 1000000, −55555
long	64-bit integer	−9223372036854775808 to 9223372036854775807	123456789000, 0, −23330333
float	32-bit floating-point number	−3.40E+38 to −1.40E−45, 0, and 1.40E−45 to 3.40E+38	2.3E+12, −3.412, 3.5E−09
double	64-bit floating-point number	−1.79E+308 to −4.940E−324, 0, and 4.94E−324 to 1.79E+308	1.233E+200, 12.345, −3.21E−88
char	Character	-	A, z, !, *, \n

The previous table shows the characters \n as an example of a character. \n is the special character for a new line that belongs to the category of escape characters. The following table shows the escape characters. These characters help you generate a special output, such as a form feed, by using characters such as \f.

Description	Escape Character
New line	\n
Horizontal tab	\t
Backspace	\b
Return	\r
Form feed	\f
Backslashes	\\
Single quote	\'

Description	Escape Character
Double quote	\"

Java indirectly supports strings of characters by using the class String to represent strings.

Variables

Java allows you to declare variables that associate names with values that can change during the execution of a Java program.

Because variables can have different values during the program execution, you can place variables in statements that assign new values for these variables. When a variable appears in an expression on the right side of an assignment operator, the variable contributes its current value to the expression. When a variable appears on the left side of an assignment operator, its value is updated by the assignment statement.

The following is an example of using variables:

```
double Sum = 0;
int i;
for(i = 1; i <= 10; i++)
   Sum = Sum + i * i;
System.out.println("Sum = " + Sum);
```

This example has the double-type variable Sum and int-type variable *i*. The example initializes the variable Sum with 0. Then the example uses a for loop that features the variable *i* as its control variable. The loop adds the square's values of the loop control variable in the variable Sum. In addition, the loop's body shows you how the variable Sum appears on both sides of the assignment operator. The occurrence of the variable Sum on the right of the = sign causes that variable to supply its current value to the expression. Then the occurrence of the variable Sum on the left of the = sign causes that variable to receive its new value. The example shows that you can repeatedly recall a value from a variable and store a new value in that variable without causing problems for the Java compiler. The previous code displays the following output:

```
Sum = 55
```

The general syntax for declaring a variable in Java is as follows:

```
dataType variableName [= initialValue];
```

This syntax indicates that the declaration of a variable includes the following parts:

+ The data type that is associated with the variable

+ The name of the variable

+ The optional value that initializes the variable

Unlike constants, Java allows you to declare variables as attributes of a class as well as local variables that are inside the methods of a class.

The following are examples of declaring variables:

```
int numDisks = 122;
double weight = 10.34;
char aChar = 'A';
```

The examples are explained as follows:

+ The first example declares the `int`-type constant `numDisks` and assigns the value of 122 to that constant.

+ The second example declares the `double`-type constant `weight` and assigns the value 10.34 to that constant.

+ The last example declares the char-type constant aChar and assigns the character *A* to that constant.

Variable Naming Rules

Java requires that you obey the following rules when you name attributes, variables, classes, methods, constants, and so on:

+ The first character must be the a letter or the underscore character.

+ Subsequent characters can be letters, digits, or the underscore character.

+ Names in Java are case-sensitive. For example `Index`, `INDEX`, and `Index` are three different names.

+ You must avoid names that Java uses. These names, like `if`, `for`, `else`, and so on, are reserved by Java.

## Part IV

Operators

Operators allow a program to query and manipulate data. In this part, I look at the various kinds of Java operators. Some operators calculate new values based on existing value. Others fiddle with the zeros and ones in data. Yet, other operators compare and query the value of data. Without operators, computers and programs become completely useless.

In this part

- ✔ Working with arithmetic operators
- ✔ Using assignment operators
- ✔ Working with bit-manipulating operators
- ✔ Using the increment and decrement operators
- ✔ Learning about operator precedence and evaluation order
- ✔ Working with relational and logical operator
- ✔ Using the `sizeof` operator

Arithmetic Operators

Arithmetic operators support the manipulation of integers and floating-point numbers. You use these operators to add, subtract, divide, and multiply numbers. The following table shows the arithmetic operators that are used in Java. A *unary operator* needs one value (also called the *operand*). By contrast, a *binary operator* requires two values (or operands).

Java Operator	Role	Data Type	Example
+	Unary plus	Numerical	$z = +h - 2$
–	Unary minus	Numerical	$z = -1 * (z + 1)$
+	Add	Numerical	$h = 34 + g$
–	Subtract	Numerical	$z = 2.4 - t$
/	Divide	Numerical	$d = m / v$
*	Multiply	Numerical	area = len * width
%	Modulus	Integer	cout = w % 12

Assignment Operators

Assignment operators (except the simple-operator) allow you to write short expressions that perform the same calculations as expressions that have the same variable appear on both sides of the = assignment operator.

The following are examples of normal expressions:

```
total = total + x;
difference = difference - x;
scale = scale / factor;
power = power * x;
```

Each of the preceding statements contains the same variable on both sides of the assignment operator. Java supports assignment operators that combine arithmetic and bitwise operations with the assignment operator (*bitwise operations* manipulate the individual bits of a value). Therefore, you can write these statements as follows:

```
total += x;
difference -= x;
scale /= factor;
power *= x;
```

The following table lists the arithmetic assignment operators in Java. The table also contains examples of using these operators in addition to the long-form versions of the statements in the examples.

Java Operator	*Example*	*Long-Form Example*
+=	fSum += fX;	fSum = fSum + fX;
-=	fY -= fX;	fY = fY – fX;
/=	nCount /= N;	nCount = nCount / N;
*=	fScl *= fFactor;	fScl = fScl * fFactor;
%=	nBins %= nCount;	nBins = nBins % nCount;

The examples in this table accomplish the following items:

+ The first example uses the += operator to add the value in variable fX to the value in variable fSum.

+ The second example uses the -= operator to subtract the value in variable fX from the value in variable fY.

+ The third example uses the /= operator to divide the value in variable nCount by the value in variable N.

+ The fourth example uses the *= operator to multiply the value in variable fScl by the value in variable fFactor.

+ The last example uses the %= operator to store in variable nBins the remainder of dividing the value in variable nBins by the value in variable nCount.

Bit-Manipulation Operators

For a programming language such as Java to be used in low-level programming, it must be able to manipulate bits quickly and efficiently. The following table shows the bit-manipulation operators that are used in Java. Note that Java supports the bitwise AND, OR, XOR, and NOT operators.

Java Operator	*Meaning*	*Example*
&	Bitwise AND	*m* & 255
|	Bitwise OR	*k* | 122
^	Bitwise XOR	*i* ^ 44
~	Bitwise NOT	~*k*
<<	Bitwise shift left	*m* << 3
>>	Bitwise shift right	*m* >> 4
>>>	Zero fill right shift	*m* >>>

The following table contains the bit-manipulation assignment operators that are used in Java.

Java Operator	Example	Long Form
&=	n &= 23	$n = n$ & 23
|=	k |= 122	$k = k$ | 122
^=	i ^= 44	$i = i$ ^ 44
+=	m += 3	$m = m + 3$
>>=	m >>= 4	$m = m$ >> 4
>>>=	m >>>= 2	$m = m$ >>> 2

Increment and Decrement Operators

Java offers the increment operators ++ and -- to support a shorthand syntax for adding or subtracting 1 from the value in a variable, respectively.

The general syntax for the operator ++ is as follows:

```
// form 1: pre-increment
++variableName
// form 2: post-increment
variableName++
```

The pre-increment version of the operator ++ increments the value in its operand `variableName` before that variable supplies its value to the host expression. By contrast, the post-increment version of the operator ++ increments the value in its operand `variableName` after that variable supplies its value to the host expression. If you use the increment operator in a statement that has no other operators (including the assignment operator), then it makes no difference which form of the operator you use. Therefore, the following two statements have the same effect:

```
nCount++;
++nCount;
```

The following are several examples of using the increment operator:

```
int nCount = 1;
int nNum;
nNum = nCount++; // nNum stores 1 and nCount
    stores 2
nNum = ++nCount; // nNum stores 3 and nCount
    stores 3
```

In this code, the variable nCount has the initial value of 1. The first statement that uses the increment operator features the post-increment version. Consequently, the statement assigns the value in variable nCount to variable nNum and then increments the value in the variable nCount. The result is that variable nNum stores 1 and variable nCount contains 2. The second statement that uses the increment operator features the pre-increment version. Consequently, the statement first increments the value in variable nCount and then assigns the value in variable nCount to the variable nNum. The result is that both variables nNum and nCount store 3.

The general syntax for the decrement operator is as follows:

```
// form 1: pre-decrement
--variableName
// form 2: post-decrement
variableName--
```

The pre-decrement version of the operator decrements the value in its operand variableName before that variable supplies its value to the host expression. By contrast, the post-decrement version of the operator decrements the value in its operand variableName after that variable supplies its value to the host expression.

If you use the decrement operator in a statement that has no other operators (including the assignment operator), then it makes no difference which form of the operator you use. Therefore, the following two statements have the same effect:

```
nCount--;
--nCount;
```

The following are some examples of using the decrement operator:

```
int nCount = 10;
int nNum;
nNum = nCount--; // nNum stores 10 and nCount
    stores 9
nNum = --nCount; // nNum stores 8 and nCount
    stores 8
```

In this code, the variable nCount has the initial value of 10. The first statement that uses the decrement operator features the post-decrement version. Consequently, the statement assigns the value in variable nCount to variable nNum and then decrements the value in the variable nCount. The result is that the variable nNum stores 10 and the variable nCount contains 9. The second statement that uses the decrement operator features the pre-decrement version. Consequently, the statement first decrements the value in variable nCount and then assigns the value in the variable nCount to the variable nNum. The result is that both nNum and nCount store 8.

Operator Precedence and Evaluation Order

If you use a simple pocket calculator, you may notice that the calculator executes the arithmetic operations in the sequence that you enter them. For example, if you press keys 2 + 4 × 10 =, you get the result 60. The calculator performs the addition and then the multiplication. In other words, all the arithmetic operators have the same priority. Programming languages, like Java, apply operator precedence when evaluating an arithmetic expression. Each operator has a precedence that determines the order of its evaluation. The following table shows the Java operators and their precedence. For example, consider the following expression:

```
X = 2 + 4 * 10;
```

This expression is evaluated by first performing the multiplication and then the addition, yielding the value of 42. To perform the addition first, you must enclose the appropriate operands in parentheses, as follows:

```
X = (2 + 4) * 10;
```

Another example is the following Boolean expression:

```
isLowercase = c >= 'a' && c <= 'z';
```

The operators >= and <= have a higher precedence than the operator &&. Therefore, the expression first compares the values using the operators >= and <= and *then* logically ANDs the result using the operator &&.

Operators	Comments
. [] ()	Dot access methods and variables. [] is used for arrays, and () is used for groups expressions.
++ -- ! ~	Increment, decrement, logical NOT, and bitwise NOT.
new	Creates class instances.
* / %	Multiplication, division, and modulus.
+ -	Addition and subtraction.
<< >> >>>	Bitwise left and right shift.
< > <= >=	Relational comparison.
== !=	Test of inequality and equality.
&	Bitwise AND.
~	Bitwise XOR.
|	Bitwise OR.
&&	Logical AND.

Operators	Comments
||	Logical OR.
?:	Conditional operator.
= += -= *= /= %= &= |= <<= >>= >>>=	Assignment operators.

Relational and Logical Operators

Programs require relational and Boolean operators to create decision-making Boolean expressions. Because decision-making is a fundamental part of programming, all common programming languages (such as BASIC, Pascal, FORTRAN, C, and C++) support these expressions.

The following table shows the relational and Boolean operators that are used in Java. Note that the list lacks the logical operator XOR. Also note that the table contains the conditional assignment operator ?:, resembling the operator ?: in C and C++, which has the following syntax:

```
(expression) ? trueValue : falseValue
```

The operator yields the trueValue if the expression is true and returns the falseValue otherwise. Therefore, you can use the conditional assignment operator to assign a value to a variable as follows:

```
variable = (expression) ? trueValue : falseValue;
```

This statement is similar to the following if statement:

```
if (expression)
  variable = trueValue;
else
  variable = falseValue;
```

Java Operator	Meaning	Example
&&	Logical AND	$k > 1$ && $k < 11$
||	Logical OR	$k < 0$ || $k > 22$
!	Logical NOT	!($k > 1$ && $k < 10$)
<	Less than	$k < 12$
<=	Less than or equal to	$k <= 33$
>	Greater than	$k > 45$

(continued)

Java Operator	Meaning	Example
>=	Greater than or equal to	$k >= 77$
==	Equal to	$k == 32$
!=	Not equal to	$k != 33$
?:	Conditional assignment	$k = (k < 0)? 1 : k$

This table shows the following examples:

◆ The example for the logical AND operator shows the condition that tests whether the value in variable k is greater than 1 and less than 11.

◆ The example for the logical OR operator shows the condition that tests whether the value in variable k is less than 0 or greater than 22.

◆ The example for the logical NOT operator shows the condition that tests whether the value in variable k is neither greater than 1 nor less than 10.

◆ The example for the operator $<$ shows the condition that tests whether the value in variable k is less than 12.

◆ The example for the operator $<=$ shows the condition that tests whether the value in variable k is less than or equal to 33.

◆ The example for the operator $>$ shows the condition that tests whether the value in variable k is greater than 45.

◆ The example for the operator $>=$ shows the condition that tests whether the value in variable k is greater than or equal to 77.

◆ The example for the operator $==$ shows the condition that tests whether the value in variable k is equal to 32.

◆ The example for the operator $!=$ shows the condition that tests whether the value in variable k is not equal to 33.

◆ The example for the conditional operator shows a statement that determines whether the value in variable k is negative. If this condition is true, the operator assigns 1 to the variable k. Otherwise, the operator assigns the value in variable k.

Boolean expressions use relational and Boolean operators to produce Boolean values. Boolean expressions can range from simple to complex. Simple expressions use one relational or Boolean operators. By contrast, complex Boolean expressions use a combination of both. The following are several examples of simple Boolean expressions:

```
i < 10
nCount >= nMinLimit
nIndex == nArrayBound
bDriveFlag && bDiskFlag
bNeedFile || bNewFile
!bNewFile
```

The examples are explained as follows:

✦ The first example tests if the variable *i* stores a number less than 10.

✦ The second example tests if the value in variable `nCount` is equal to or greater than the value in the variable `nMinLimit`.

✦ The third example tests if the values in variables `nIndex` and `nArrayBound` are equal.

✦ The fourth example tests if the logical values in variables `bDriveFlag` and `bDiskFlag` are both true.

✦ The fifth example tests if the value in either variable `bNeedFile` or `bNewFile` is true.

✦ The last example tests if the logical value in the variable `bNewFile` is false.

The following are some examples of more complex Boolean expressions:

```
i < 10 && i >= 100
!(nCount < nMinLimit || nCount > nMaxLimit)
nIndex >= nArrayBound && nIndex < 100
```

The examples are explained as follows:

✦ The first example tests if the value in variable *i* is in the range of 10 to 99.

✦ The second example determines whether the value of variable `nCount` is not outside the range defined by the variables `nMinLimit` and `nMaxLimit`.

✦ The last example tests if the value in variable `nIndex` is in the range of the value in `nArrayBound` to 99.

When you write a Boolean expression, make sure that the expression is neither consistently true nor consistently false. This kind of consistency robs a program from true decision-making. For example, consider the following expression:

```
nCount < 0 && nCount > 100
```

This Boolean expression is always false, because the value in the variable `nCount` cannot be negative and exceed 100.

Sizeof Operator

Frequently, your programs need to know the byte size of a data type or a variable in order to manage storing data of that type or storing that variable. Java provides the sizeof operator, which takes for an argument either a data type or the name of a variable (scalar, array, class instance, and so on).

The general syntax for the sizeof operator is as follows:

```
sizeof({variable_name | data_type})
sizeof {variable_name | data_type}
```

The following are examples of using the sizeof operator:

```
int sizeDifference = sizeof(double) -
    sizeof(float);
int intSize = sizeof int;
```

This example declares the variable sizeDifference and initializes this variable using the expression sizeof(double) - sizeof(float). The expression applies the sizeof operator to the predefined data types double and float. This example also declares the variable intSize and initializes it with the result of applying the sizeof operator to the type int.

## Part V

Decision-Making Constructs

Making decisions empowers programs to examine program values and determine which course of action to take. Without decision-making features, programs perform only trivial tasks. This part shows you the if and switch statements in Java and indicate how to use them to make decisions. The section for the if statement indicates that you can perform simple or complex decisions with that statement.

In this part

🖝 Working with the if statement

🖝 Using the switch statement

The if Statement

Java offers different versions of the if statement to offer decision-making with varying levels of sophistication. These levels are related to the number of alternate routes of action. The simplest form of the if statement offers a single alternative: When a condition is true, do the following tasks. The dual-alternative form of the if statement gives you two alternatives. Finally, the most sophisticated form of the if statement supports multiple alternatives.

The simple if statement

Java offers the simple if statement to support single-alternative decision-making. The general syntax for the simple if statement is as follows:

```
// form 1
if (condition)
statement;
// form 2
if (condition) {
sequence of statement
}
```

The if statement uses the key word *if* followed by the parentheses that contain the tested condition. If that condition is true, the program executes the statement (see form 1) or the block of statements (see form 2) that come after the tested condition. Otherwise, the program bypasses the statement (or block of statements) that appears after the tested condition.

The following are examples of the single-alternative if statement:

```
// example 1
if (nNum < 0)
System.out.println("Value is negative!");

// example 2
if (i > 0 && i <= 100)
System.out.println("Number is in range 1 to 100");

// example 3
if (nCount < 1)
nCount = 1;
```

These examples are explained as follows:

+ The first example uses the if statement to display a message if the value in the variable nNum is negative.

+ The second example uses the if statement to display a message when the variable *i* contains an integer between 1 and 100.

◆ The third example assigns 1 to the variable nCount if that variable contains a value that is less than 1.

The if-else statement

Java enables the if statement to support dual-alternative decision-making. The general syntax for the dual-alternative if statement is as follows:

```
if (condition)
    statement or block of statements
else
    statement or block of statements
```

The dual-alternative if statement uses the key word *else* to separate the two sets of statements that offer the alternate action. If the tested condition is true, the program executes the statement or statement block that comes after the tested condition. Otherwise, program execution resumes after the key word *else* and executes the subsequent statement or statement block.

The following are some examples of the dual-alternative if statement:

```
// example 1
if (nNum < 0)
System.out.println("Value is negative");
else
System.out.println("Value is 0 or greater");

// example 2
if (i > 0 && i <= 100)
j = i * i;
else
j = 100;

// example 3
if (nCount < 1)
nCount = 1
else
nCount-;
```

These examples are explained as follows:

◆ The first example uses the if statement to determine whether the value in variable nNum is negative. If this condition is true, the program displays the message Value is negative. Otherwise, the program executes the statement in the else clause to display the message Value is 0 or greater.

◆ The second example uses the if statement to determine whether the variable *i* contains an integer between 1 and 100. If this condition is true, the program assigns the expression i * i to the variable *j*. Otherwise, the program executes the else clause statement to assign 100 to the variable *j*.

✦ The third example uses the if statement to determine whether the value in variable nCount is less than 1. If this condition is true, the program assigns 1 to the variable nCount. Otherwise, the program executes the else clause statement to decrement the value in the variable nCount.

The multiple-alternative if statement

Java also permits the if statement to support multiple-alternative decision-making by nesting if statements. The general syntax for the multiple-alternative if statement is as follows:

```
if (condition1)
    statement #1 or block of statements #1
else if (condition2)
    statement #2 or block of statements #2
else if (condition3)
    statement #3 or block of statements #3
    ...
    other else if clauses
    ...
else
    catch-all statement or catch-all block of state-
    ments
```

The multiple-alternative if statement allows you to test a battery of conditions and take one of several courses of action. Note that the if statement tests the Boolean expressions condition1, condition2, condition3, and so on, in that sequence. The first condition that is true causes the runtime system to execute the statements that are associated with that condition. Then the program execution resumes after the if statement. If none of the tested conditions are true, the program executes the statements in the catch-all else clause (if one is used).

The following is an example of a multiple-alternative if statement:

```
if (N >= 0 && N < 10)
    System.out.println("Variable N is a single
    digit");
else if (N >= 10 && N < 100)
    System.out.println("Variable N has two digits");
else if (N >= 100 && N < 1000)
    System.out.println("Variable N has three dig-
    its");
else if (N >= 1000)
    System.out.println("Variable N has four digits");
else
    System.out.println("Variable N is negative");
```

This code classifies the value in variable *N*. The condition of the if clause determines whether the variable *N* contains an integer from 0 to 9. The first else if clause determines whether the variable *N* contains an integer from 10 to 99. Then the second else if clause determines whether the variable *N* contains an integer from 100 to 999. Finally, the third else if clause determines whether the variable *N* contains an integer that is equal to or greater than 1000. Each of the if and else if clauses displays a message reflecting the value in the variable *N*. The else clause displays the message that the variable *N* contains a negative value.

TIP

To speed the execution of a multiple-alternative if statement, arrange the tested conditions in the order that they're likely to be true. In other words, place the condition that is most likely to be true in the first if clause and the condition least likely to be true in the last if else clause.

The switch Statement

SYNTAX

Java offers the switch statement to support multiple-alternative decision-making. The general syntax for the multiple-alternative switch statement is as follows:

```
switch(expression)
{
  case constantExpression1:
    statements set #1
    break;
  case constantExpression2:
    statements set #2
    break;
...
[default:
  catch-all statements]
}
```

The switch statement examines the value of the expression, which must be an integer or be integer-compatible (the list of valid data types includes byte, short, int, and char). The condition of the switch statement can be a variable, a method call, or an expression that includes constants, variables, and the results of invoking a method.

The switch statement uses case labels for comparing the tested expression with different values. Java has the following rules about case labels:

✦ The key word *case* is followed by a single constant (either a literal constant or a constant expression), which is then followed by a colon.

✦ You can include a sequence of several case labels that execute the same sequence of statements.

✦ A case label cannot list a range of constant values. Each case label lists only one constant.

The program execution sequentially examines the values in the case labels. If a case label value matches the tested expression, the program executes the statements that come after the case label. To prevent the program from examining remaining case labels (after it finds a matching value), use the break statement. This statement causes the program flow to jump to the end of the switch statement.

Here is an example for a method that uses a switch statement to convert the argument of a char-type parameter into an integer code and then return that code:

```
int getCode(char Letter)
{
    int result;

    switch (Letter) {
        case 'a':
            result = 1;

        case 'b':
            result = 2;

        case 'c':
            result = 3;

        default:
            result = -1;
    }
    return result;
}
```

The preceding example shows the method getCode(), which returns an integer based on the argument for the char-type parameter Letter. The method uses a switch statement to examine the value of parameter Letter. Each case label is followed by a statement that assigns a value to the local variable result. The last statement in the method has a return statement that returns the value in variable result.

## Part VI

Loops

Loops allow your programs to repeat (that is, iterate) one or more statements to perform a task. One of the main advantages of computers over people is the ability of computers to repeat tasks correctly and tirelessly. This part covers the three loops in Java and shows you how to nest loops. You also can find out how to exit loops prematurely and how to skip part of a loop iteration.

In this part

✔ **Using the** do-while **loop.**

✔ **Using the** for **loop**

✔ **Working with the** while **loop**

✔ **Nesting loops**

✔ **Exiting loops**

✔ **Skipping loop iterations**

The do-while Loop

Fixed-iteration loops are suitable when you know how many times you want to repeat a set of statements. In many cases, though, you can't determine the number of iterations. That's where conditional loops come in handy. Conditional loops iterate while a tested condition is true, allowing the number of iterations to vary significantly if necessary.

Java offers two conditional loops: the do-while and the while loops. The do-while loop iterates as long as a tested condition (located after the while clause) is true. The syntax for the do-while loop is as follows:

```
do {
    statements
} while (condition);
```

The syntax of the do-while loop shows that the loop tests the iteration condition after executing the loop's statement. Therefore, the do-while loop executes at least once.

The following is an example of the do-while loop:

```
do {
    nNum = Math.nextInt();
} while (nNum < 1);
```

This example has a do-while loop that iterates as long as the random number generated by the method Math.nextInt() and stored in the variable nNum is less than 1.

Exiting Loops

Java gives you the option to make an early exit from a loop and skip executing the remaining statements. Why do that? In some cases, you may no longer need to execute the remaining loop statements. You also can use the break statement to exit the do-while and while loops. By default, the break statement exits the current loop (or switch statement). Java allows you to place a label to explicitly guide the jump with a break statement. This feature allows you to exit nested loops.

The general syntax for using the break statement with a label is as follows:

```
outer loop begins here
...
inner loop begins here
...
```

```
if (condition)
  break label
...
inner loop ends here
...
outer loop ends here
...
label:
...
```

Using labels to guide a program jump seems to resurrect the goto statement, so you may want to avoid using this programming feature.

The following are some examples of using the break statement with the do-while and while loops:

```
// exit from do-while loop example
double fY, fX = 1.0;
do {
  fY = fX * fX + 10;
  if (fY > 10000.0)
    break;
  System.out.println("f(" + fX + ") = " + fY);
} while (fX < 100.0);

// exit from while loop example
double fY, fX = 1.0;
while (fX > 0.0 && fX < 100.0) {
  fY = fX * fX - 30;
  System.out.println("f(" + fX + ") = " + fY);
  if (fY > 1000.0)
    break;
};
```

The first example has a do-while loop, which iterates as long as the value in variable fX is less than 100. Then the loop contains a statement that determines whether the value in the variable fY (which is based on the value of variable fX) exceeds 10000. If this condition is true, the loop exits by executing the break statement in the if statement.

The second example has a while loop, which iterates as long as the value in variable fX is positive and less than 100. The loop contains an if statement that determines whether the value in the variable fY (which is based on the value of variable fX) exceeds 1000. If this condition is true, the loop exits by executing the break statement in the if statement.

The for Loop

Java offers the fixed-iteration `for` loop, which was influenced by the C and C++ programming language. The general syntax for the `for` loop is as follows:

```
for (initializationPart; continuationPart;
    updatePart);
```

The `for` loop contains the following three parts:

◆ The *initialization part* initializes the loop control variables. You can use single or multiple loop control variables.

◆ The *continuation part* contains a Boolean expression that causes the loop to iterate as long as the expression is true.

◆ The *update part* increments or decrements the loop control variables.

The following are some examples of the `for` loop:

```
// example 1
for (i = 0; i < 10; i++)
    System.out.println(i);

// example 2
for (i = 9; i >= 0; i -= 3)
    System.out.println((i*i));

// example 3
for (int i = 1; i < 100; i++)
    System.out.println(i);

// example 4
for (int i = 0, j = MAX; i < j; i++, j-)
System.out.println(i + 2 * j);
```

These examples are explained as follows:

◆ The first example initializes the loop control variable *i* to 0 and iterates as long as the value in the variable *i* is less than 10. The loop update part increases the value of the variable *i* by 1. Therefore, the upward-counting loop iterates ten times, with the value in the variable *i* changing from 0 to 9.

◆ The second examples shows a downward-counting loop, which initializes the loop control variable *i* to 9. This loop iterates as long as the value in the variable *i* is not negative. The loop update part decreases the value of the variable *i* by 3. Therefore, the loop iterates four times with the value in the variable *i* having the sequence 9, 6, 3, and 0.

✦ The third example shows an interesting programming feature that is related to the `for` loop. This example declares the loop control variable *i* and initializes it to 1. The loop iterates as long as the value in the variable *i* is less than 100. Note that the loop update part increases the value of the variable *i* by 1. Therefore, the upward-counting loop iterates 99 times with the value in the variable *i* changing from 1 to 99.

✦ The fourth example shows that a `for` loop can declare and initialize multiple loop control variables. The loop initializes the variables *i* and *j* to 0 and `MAX`, respectively. This loop also iterates as long as the value in the variable *i* is less than that in the variable *j*. The loop update part increases the value in each of the variables *i* and *j* by 1.

Nesting Loops

Loops are suitable for steps that need to be executed repeatedly. In many cases, a main task has a set of tasks that need to be repeated, and one or more tasks have subtasks that need to be repeated. A good analogy of nested loops is an analog watch with a small hand and a large hand. The large hand turns 24 times a day (that's like 24 iterations of a loop) and causes the small hand to turn 2 times (that's 2 iterations).

Like other common programming languages, Java allows you to nest loops in any combination. For example, you can nest `for` loops, as shown in the following example:

```
double fSum = 0;
for (int i = 10; i < 100; i++)
   for (int j = 0; j < i; j++)
      fSum += double(j * i);
```

This code shows two nested `for` loops that are used to obtain a sum.

You can also nest different kinds of loops. The following code shows nested `while` and `do-while` loops:

```
double fSum = 0;
int i = 10;
int j;
while (i < 100) {
   j = 0;
     do {
       fSum += j++ * i;
     } while (j < i);
     i++;
}
```

The nested loops obtain a sum, like the one in the example of the nested `for` loops.

Skipping Loop Iterations

In addition to exiting a loop at a certain statement in that loop, you also can exit the loop and resume the next iteration. This condition arises when you should not execute the remaining set of statements in a loop but need to resume starting with the loop's first statement.

Java offers the `continue` statement to skip the remaining statements in a loop. Why skip the remaining loop statements? This condition arises when the loop statements examine a condition and conclude that the loop should not or need not proceed with executing the remaining statements.

The following is an example of using the `continue` statement:

```
for (int i = -4; i < 5; i++) {
  if (i == 0)
continue;
    double fX =  1.0 / i;
    System.out.println("1 / " + i + " = " + fX);
}
```

This code shows a loop that displays reciprocal values. The loop has a control variable that changes values from –4 to 4 in increments of 1. This loop contains an if statement that determines whether the control variable contains 0. When this condition is true, the loop skips the remaining statements to avoid dividing by zero.

Java allows you to direct the program jump of a `continue` statement by using a label. When you use this feature, you can resume the next iteration at a location other than the beginning of the current loop. The general syntax for using the `continue` statement with a label is as follows:

```
loop begins here
...
label:
...
if (condition)
  continue label
...
loop ends here
```

Because this method seems to resurrect the `goto` statement, you may want to avoid using labels to guide a program jump.

## Part VII

Classes

This part gives you information on working with classes. In this part, you find out about the role of a class and how to declare a base class and a hierarchy of classes. This part also looks at the access levels of class components as well as the role of static attributes. Morever, this part covers working with abstract classes as well as handling runtime errors using exceptions.

In this part

- ✔ Working with abstract classes
- ✔ Finding out about access levels of a class
- ✔ Working with base classes
- ✔ Creating class hierarchies
- ✔ Finding out about classes
- ✔ Using constructors
- ✔ Using exceptions to handle runtime errors
- ✔ Working with static attributes

Abstract Classes

Suppose that you're the head of a programming team (you were promoted just for reading this book!) and need to define the declaration of methods for other programmers to implement. Wouldn't it be great if you could declare a general or abstract class that contains just the definitions of methods? The programmers who work under your guidance would then derive new classes that fully implement the abstract methods.

Well, the good news is that many object-oriented programming languages (such as C++ and Java) support a formal syntax to make this programming feature possible. Java allows you to declare classes as abstract by using the modifier abstract. An abstract class has the following features:

✦ The declaration of the class includes the modifier abstract, which appears before the key word *class.*

✦ You cannot create instances of an abstract class.

✦ The class declares at least one method as abstract, using the modifier abstract. An abstract method does not have a body of statements that defines it.

✦ The descendant classes must define the abstract methods of the parent abstract class.

✦ The declaration of the abstract class may contain attributes and nonabstract methods if these attributes and methods can be inherited by the descendant classes.

An abstract class is usually at the root of a class hierarchy. You can declare abstract classes as descendants of nonabstract classes. In other words, an abstract class can become the root of a class subhierarchy. You can also declare multiple generations of descendant classes that are abstract. In this case, the *granddaddy* of these abstract classes contains the most general declarations, compared to its descendant abstract classes.

The following is an example of an abstract class and its nonabstract descendant class:

```
abstract class TV {
   abstract public void turnOn();
   abstract public void turnOff();
   abstract public void selectChannel(int nChannel);
   abstract public void selectVolume(int nVolume);
}

class myTV extends TV {
   protected boolean m_bIsOn;
   protected int m_nChannel;
```

```
protected int m_nVolume;

public void turnOn() {
  m_bIsOn = true;
}

public void turnOff() {
  m_bIsOn = true;
}

public void selectChannel(int nChannel) {
  m_nChannel = nChannel;
}

public void selectVolume(int nVolume) {
  m_nVolume = nVolume;
}
}
```

This example shows the abstract class TV and its nonabstract descendant class myTV. The class TV declares the abstract methods turnOn(), turnOff(), setChannel(), and setVolume(). These methods turn on the TV, turn off the TV, set the channel, and set the volume, respectively.

The descendant class declares the following attributes:

✦ The boolean-type attribute m_bIsOn stores the on/off mode.

✦ The int-type attribute m_nChannel stores the TV channel number.

✦ The int-type attribute m_nVolume stores the volume level.

The descendant class declares the fully defined methods turnOn(), turnOff(), setChannel(), and setVolume(). These methods define the abstract methods that are inherited from the parent class.

If a class that is a descendant of an abstract class doesn't define all the abstract methods that are inherited from the parent class, the compiler regards the descendant class as also being abstract.

Access Levels of a Class

The evolution from structured programming to object-oriented programming has enabled more sophisticated aspects of controlling the access of classes and their components. Java (like C++) supports sophisticated access schemes that allow you to limit the access of a class altogether or limit some of its attributes and/or methods. The key words *public, protected,* and *private* (which are part of a special set of key words called *class modifiers*) should give you a good clue of the access level of the attributes and methods that are associated with these class modifiers.

The public level

The modifier public tells the Java compiler that the attribute or method that is associated with that modifier can be accessed by class instances, other classes, and instances of other classes. In other words, the modifier public removes any access restrictions.

The following is an example of a class that only has public attributes and methods:

```
public class myInt
{
  public int m_nInt = 0;
  public long getSquare() {
    return m_nInt * m_nInt;
  }

  public static void main(String args[]) {
    myInt intObj = new myInt();

    intObj.m_nInt = 5;
    System.out.println(intObj.m_nInt + "squared = "
+
                       intObj.getSquare());
  }
}
```

This version of class myInt declares the public int-type attribute m_nInt as well as the public methods getSquare() and (as always) main(). The method getSquare() returns the squared value of the attribute m_nInt. The method main() performs the following tasks:

✦ Declares the object intObj as an instance of class myInt.

✦ Assigns the value 5 to the attribute m_nInt of object intObj. This task assigns the integer value directly to the attribute, because the latter is public.

✦ Displays the value in attribute m_nInt of object intObj and its squared value. This task also accesses the attribute m_nInt directly to obtain its value. Moreover, this task returns the squared value by sending the message getSquare() to object intObj.

The protected level

Java allows you to declare protected attributes and methods. When you use the protected modifier, you deny access to these class components by the class instances. Programming gurus recommend that you typically declare attributes as *protected* to keep them from direct access by class instances. This kind of access may corrupt the values in these attributes and disrupt the state of the class instances.

How do you declare a method as protected? You typically do this if that method is an auxiliary one — that is, the protected method is one that works exclusively for other methods in the class and should not be sent as a message to a class instance.

The following is an example of a class that has protected attributes and methods:

```
public class myPositiveInt
{
  protected int m_nInt = 1;

  public boolean setInt(int nInt) {
    boolean isOk = checkInt(nInt)

    if (isOk)
      m_nInt = nInt;
    return isOk;
  }

  public int getInt() {
    return m_nInt;
  }

  protected boolean checkInt(int nInt) {
    return nInt > 0;
  }

  public static void main(String args[]) {
    myPositiveInt intObj = new myPositiveInt();

    intObj.setInt(5);
    System.out.println("Object intObj store " +
      intObj.getInt());
  }
}
```

The class myPositiveInt declares the protected int-type attribute m_nInt, the protected method checkInt(), and the public methods setInt(), getInt(), and main(). The class declares the following methods:

+ The boolean method checkInt() examines the value in its int-type parameter nInt and returns true if that value is positive. Otherwise, the method yields false.

+ The method setInt() stores the value of its int-type parameter nInt in the attribute m_nInt when the value of the parameter is positive. The method setInt() uses the protected method checkInt() to verify the value of the parameter nInt. Therefore, the method checkInt is an auxiliary method that works exclusively for the method setInt().

+ The method getInt() returns the value in the attribute m_nInt.

The method `main()` performs the following tasks:

✦ Declares the object `intObj` as an instance of class `myPositiveInt`.

✦ Assigns the value 5 to the object `intObj`. This task sends the message `setInt()` to the object `intObj`.

✦ Displays the integer that is stored in the object `intObj`.

✦ Sends the message `getInt()` to that object.

The private level

Java allows you to declare private attributes and methods. When you use the `private` modifier, you deny access to these class components by the class instances and descendant classes that are declared in other files. Programming gurus recommend that you typically declare attributes as *private* when you consider their data to be too sensitive to be accessed by even descendant classes.

How do you declare methods as private? You typically do this if that method is an auxiliary one and works on private attributes. In other words, private methods work in concert with private attributes.

The following is an example of a class that has private attributes and methods:

```
public class MyPositiveInt
{
  private int m_nInt = 1;

  public boolean setInt(int nInt) {
    boolean isOk = checkInt(nInt)

    if (isOk)
      m_nInt = nInt;
    return isOk;
  }

  public int getInt() {
    return m_nInt;
  }

  private boolean checkInt(int nInt) {
    return nInt > 0;
  }

  public static void main(String args[]) {
    myPositiveInt intObj = new myPositiveInt();
```

(continued)

(continued)
```
      intObj.setInt(5);
      System.out.println("Object intObj store " +
         intObj.getInt());
   }
}
```

This source code is a version of the class `myPositiveInt` that uses a private (instead of protected) attribute and a private method. The class otherwise performs the same tasks as the previous version. This example shows you that, for a single class, the protected and private modifiers have the same effect. The difference between these modifiers appears when you create descendant classes.

Base Classes

Java supports declaring classes that encapsulate attributes and methods. The attributes (also called *class variables*) store values that represent the state of the class instances (that is, the objects that belong to the class). The methods set and query the state of the class instances by manipulating the values in the attributes.

The general syntax for declaring a base class in Java is as follows:

```
class className {
    zero or more attributes
    zero or more methods
}
```

Declaring a class starts with the key word *class,* followed by the name of the class. The declaration of the class includes the attributes and the methods. You can initialize the attributes of a class, but you must fully implement the methods of a class within the class declaration.

The following is an example of a class that encapsulates integers:

```
class myInt
{
  protected int m_nInt = 0;

public void setInt(int nNewNum) {
    m_nInt = nNewNum;
    }
public int getInt() {
    return m_nInt;
    }
public void show(String Message) {
    System.out.println(Message + m_nInt);
    }
```

This code declares the class my Int, which encapsulates int-type integers. The class has one attribute and three methods. The class declares the protected int-type attribute m_nInt, which stores the integer; it also declares the following public methods:

✦ The method setInt() copies the value of the parameter nNewNum into the attribute m_nInt.

✦ The method getInt() returns the value of the attribute m_nInt.

✦ The method show() displays the value in the attribute m_nInt.

Class Hierarchy

Java allows you to declare a descendant class from a parent class. The general syntax for declaring a descendant class that uses the single inheritance scheme is as follows:

```
class className extends parentClassName
{
    zero or more attributes
    zero or more methods
}
```

Declaring a descendant class starts with the key word *class* and is followed by the name of the descendant class, the key word *extends,* and then the name of the parent class. The key word *extends* tells the Java compiler that the className is a descendant of the parent class. Note that the descendant class adds new attributes and/or methods that are inherited from the parent class. The declaration of the class includes these new attributes and methods. The attributes of the descendant class are added to the ones that are inherited from the parent classes and must not have the same names as the inherited ones. Note that the descendant class declares new methods as well as methods that override inherited ones. You can initialize the attributes when you declare them, but you must fully implement the methods.

The constructors of a descendant class need to use the parameterless constructor of the parent class. This kind of usage is automatic. Therefore, make sure that the parent classes (and preferably all classes) have parameterless constructors.

Java enforces the following rules regarding the public, protected, and private attributes as well as the methods of a descendant class:

✦ All the methods can access all the attributes in a class, regardless of their access level.

♦ The class instances can only access the public attributes and methods.

♦ The methods of a descendant class can only access public and protected attributes and/or methods of the parent class. Therefore, the private attributes and/or methods of a class cannot be accessed by the methods of a descendant class.

The following is an example of declaring a parent class and a descendant class:

```
class Rectangle
{
  protected double m_fLength = 0;
  protected double m_fWidth = 0;

  public Rectangle()
      { setDimensions(0, 0); }

  public Rectangle(double fLength, double fWidth)
      { setDimensions(fLength, fWidth); }
  public void setDimensions(double fLength,
                            double fWidth) {
    m_fLength = fLength;
    m_fWidth = fWidth;
  }
  public double getLength() {
    return m_fLength;
  }
  public double getWidth() {
    return m_fWidth;
  }
  public double getArea() {
    return m_fLength * m_fWidth;
  }
}

class Solid extends Rectangle {
  protected double m_fHeight = 0;
  public Solid(double fLength, double fWidth,
          double fHeight) {
    setDimensions(fLength, fWidth, fHeight);
  }
  public void setDimensions(double fLength,
      double fWidth, double fHeight) {
    m_fLength = fLength;
    m_fWidth = fWidth;
    m_fHeight = fHeight;
  }
  public double getHeight() {
    return m_fHeight;
  }
  public double getVolume(){
    return m_fHeight * getArea();
  }
}
```

This example declares the class Rectangle and its descendant class Solid. The class Rectangle, which represents a simple rectangle, declares the protected double-type attributes m_fLength and m_fWidth. These attributes store the length and width of a rectangle, respectively. The class declares the following public constructors and methods:

+ Two constructors initialize the attributes. The first constructor, Rectangle(), assigns zeros to the attributes. The second constructor, Rectangle(double fLength, double fWidth), assigns the values of the parameters fLength and fWidth to the attributes m_fLength and m_fWidth, respectively.

+ The method setDimensions() assigns new values to the attributes.

+ The method getLength() returns the value in the attribute m_fLength.

+ The method getWidth() returns the value in the attribute m_fWidth.

+ The method getArea() returns the area of the rectangle, which is calculated by using the attributes.

The example also declares the class Solid, which represents a simple solid shape, as a descendant of the class Rectangle. The descendant class declares the protected double-type attribute m_fHeight, which stores the height of the solid. Then the class inherits the protected attributes m_fLength and m_fWidth and ends up with three attributes. The class Solid also declares the following public constructor and methods:

+ The constructor Solid(double fLength, double fWidth, double fHeight) initializes the attributes. This constructor automatically uses the parameterless constructor of the parent class. Therefore, the class Rectangle needs this kind of constructor to work with the constructor of the class Solid.

+ The method setDimensions() assigns new values to the attributes. This method is a new version that assigns values to the inherited and declared attributes.

+ The method getHeight() returns the value in the attribute m_fHeight.

+ The method getVolume() returns the volume of the solid shape, which is calculated by using the attribute m_fHeight and the result of the inherited method getArea().

The class Solid inherits the methods setDimensions(double, double) (the one that assigns values to the inherited attributes), getLength(), getWidth(), and getArea(). The definition of method getVolume() uses the inherited method getArea().

Constructors

Constructors are special methods that initialize the class instances. Java allows you to declare one or more constructors in a class to allow you to initialize the class instances in one of many ways. The constructor has the same name as the class and has no return type. Typically, you declare a constructor as public to allow any method to use it. The constructor may have an empty parameter list, or it may have one or more parameters.

The following is an example of a class that encapsulates integers and uses constructors:

```
class myInt
{
  protected int m_nInt;

  // constructors
  public myInt() {
    m_nInt = 0;
  }
  public myInt(int nInt) {
    m_nInt = nInt;
  }
  public myInt(myInt anObj) {
    m_nInt = anObj.getInt();
  }
public void setInt(int nNewNum) {
    m_nInt = nNewNum;
  }
public int getInt() {
    return m_nInt;
  }
public void show(String Message) {
    System.out.println(Message + m_nInt);
  }
}
```

This code declares a version of the class myInt, which contains the following constructors:

✦ The first constructor is parameterless and initializes the attribute m_nInt with 0.

✦ The second constructor has the int-type parameter nInt. The constructor uses the argument for this parameter to initialize the attribute m_nInt.

♦ The third constructor has the myInt-type parameter anObj (that is, an instance of the class myInt) and initializes the attribute m_nInt with the result of sending the message getInt() to object anObj.

The following are several examples of using these constructors to create instances of the class myInt:

```
Int1 = new myInt();
Int2 = new myInt(10);
Int3 = new myInt(Int2);
```

These examples create the following instances:

♦ The object Int1 is created using the first constructor. The attribute m_nInt for this object is initially 0.

♦ The object Int2 is created using the second constructor, using the integer value 10. The attribute m_nInt for this object is initially 10.

♦ The object Int3 is created using the third constructor, which uses an existing instance of the class myInt (in this case, the instance Int2). The attribute m_nInt for this object is initially 10.

See the "Creating Class Instances" subheading in the section "Base Classes."

Exceptions

Java supports exceptions and exception handling to detect and manage runtime errors. The word *exception* comes from the *exceptional program flow* that occurs during a runtime error.

Java makes use of classes and objects in handling exceptions. The terms used in Java to handle exceptions are *throwing* and *catching* exceptions; either the runtime or your code throws exceptions. To handle the thrown exceptions, you need to catch these exceptions and handle them.

Objects allocated to catch the thrown exceptions must be a subclass of Throwable (or one of its descendant classes). This class has two important descendants, Error and Exception, which assist in managing various kinds of errors and exceptions.

The classes Throwable, Error, and Exception form the foundation of the exception-handling subhierarchy in Java. The classes Error and Exception form separate subhierarchies, yet behave similarly to the exception-related statements.

`Error` and `Exception` form separate subhierarchies, yet behave similarly to the exception-related statements.

Exception classes

Java makes use of classes to represent and encapsulate exceptions. All exceptions must be the descendant of the class `Throwable` (or any of its descendants, such as `Error` and `Exception`). Two general kinds of classes model exceptions:

+ **Skeleton classes:** These classes have no attributes because their names are sufficient to refer to and handle the exception.

+ **Classes with attributes:** These classes declare attributes that allow them to better describe the exception.

The following are examples of exception classes:

```
class badInputException extends Throwable {}
class badRangeException extends Exception {}
class badFileException extends Error {
  public String m_Filename;
}
```

The first two examples are skeleton classes that model exception-handling input and a range of values; these classes have no attributes. The last example declares an exception class that has the attribute `m_Filename`. This class supposedly uses this attribute to describe the file that failed a file I/O operation. Note that the exception classes `badInputException`, `badRangeException`, and `badFileException` are descendants of the classes `Throwable`, `Exception`, and `Error`, respectively.

Throwing an exception

Java offers the `throw` statement to throw an exception (an instance of an exception class). The general syntax for the `throw` statement is as follows:

```
throw exceptionObject;
```

The `exceptionObject` is an exception class instance. The latter can be a previously declared instance or a temporary instance created using both the operator `new` and the constructor of the exception class.

The following are several examples of throwing exceptions:

```
class badValueException extends Throwable{
  public  badValueException(int nVal) {
    System.out.println(nVal + " is a bad value");
  }
```

(continued)

(continued)

```
}
class ErrorDemo {
  public static void main(String arguments[]) {
    badValueException ERR = new badValueException(-1);
    ...
    throw ERR;
    ...
  }
}
```

This code shows a `throw` statement that throws an instance of the exception class `badValueException`. Note that I have not yet introduced the `try` statement, which should contain the `throw` statement. I have also not introduced the `catch` statement, which catches the exceptions.

The try block

Throwing an exception occurs in a `try` block, which causes the compiler to pay special attention to generating code for handling exceptions. The general syntax for the `try` block is as follows:

```
try {
  statements that may throw one or more exceptions
}
```

The `try` block contains any statement that may raise an exception, including `throw` statements. The following is an example of a `try` block:

```
class badValueException extends Throwable{
  public  badValueException(int nVal) {
    System.out.println(nVal + " is a bad value");
  }
}

class ErrorDemo {
  public static void main(String arguments[]) {
    badValueException ERR = new badValueException(-1);
    ...
    try {
      ...
      throw ERR;
    }
    // statements to handle the exception
    ...
  }
}
```

This code shows a `try` block that contains a `throw` statement. The statements that follow the `try` block handle the exceptions that are raised in the `try` block. The next section discusses the exception-handing `catch` handler.

The catch clause

Java offers the `catch` clauses (or handlers) to work with the `try` block. The `catch` handlers have a logic similar to that of the `case` clauses of a `switch` statement. The general syntax for a catch handler is as follows:

```
catch(exceptionType exceptionObject) {
  statements that handle or rethrow the exception
}
```

A `catch` clause declares an exception type and an exception parameter. You need this parameter to pass additional information that is related to the exception. You can use multiple `catch` handlers to catch and handle exceptions, as shown in the following general syntax:

```
catch(exceptionType1 exceptionObject1) {
  statements that handle or rethrow exceptionType1
}
catch(exceptionType2 exceptionObject2) {
  statements that handle or rethrow the
    exceptionType2
}
catch(exceptionType3 exceptionObject3) {
  statements that handle or rethrow the
    exceptionType3
}
...
[catch(Throwable t) {
  statements that handle or rethrow all other
    exceptions
}]
```

Note that this syntax shows an optional `catch` clause that uses the class `Throwable`. This kind of clause acts as a catch-all clause. Languages such as C++ support formal catch-all clauses; however, Java does not. The catch clause `catch(Throwable t)` is, in effect, a catch-all clause. This clause catches all descendents of the class `Throwable`. I recommend that you place this kind of `catch` clause at the very end of a set of `catch` clauses.

The `catch` clause `catch(Throwable t)` is a catch-all clause. Use this catch-all handler carefully; it can cause errors that you did not anticipate!

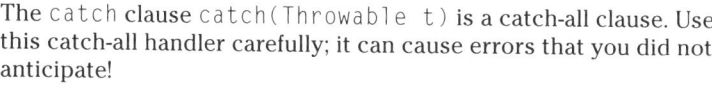

The following is an example of using the `try` block with the `catch` clauses:

```
class myError1 extends Exception {};
class myError2 extends Exception {
  public int m_nError;
  public myError2(int nError) {
    m_nError = nError;
```

(continued)

(continued)
```
    }
}

class AAA {
  public static void main(String args[]) {

    int nVal = -1;

    try {
      throw new myError2(nVal);
    }
    catch(myError1 e1)
    {
      System.out.println("Handling myError1
    exception");
    }
    catch(myError2 e2)
    {
      System.out.println("Handling myError2 excep-
    tion: "
        + "value " + e2.m_nError + " is invalid");
    }
    catch(Throwable t) {
      System.out.println("Handling other errors");
    }
  }
}
```

This example declares the exception classes myError1 and
myError2. Both classes are descendants of the class Exception.
The first exception class is a skeleton class, whereas the second
class has the public attribute m_nError. Note that the class
myError2 has a constructor that initializes the attribute
m_nError. The method main() declares and initializes the int-
type variable nVal. Then the method has a try block, which
contains a throw statement that throws a myError2 exception
(using the value in the variable nVal). The method main() has
the following catch clauses:

✦ The catch(myError1 e1) clause catches myError1 exceptions.
This clause has no parameter and simply displays a message.

✦ The catch(myError2 e2) clause catches myError2
exceptions. This clause displays a message and then displays
the attribute e2.m_nError. This clause shows you how to use
the exception parameter.

✦ The catch(Throwable t) clause catches all exceptions
other than myError1 and myError2.

The best way to arrange catch clauses is to start with those
clauses that handle more specific errors. In addition, Java requires
you to place the descendant exception classes before their parents
in the catch clauses.

Nested try-catch block

When you handle sophisticated exceptions, you may wonder about nesting try blocks and catch clauses inside other catch clauses. Java allows you to nest try blocks. In other words, you can throw a new exception while handling another one. The nature of such an action depends on the first exception that you are handling.

The following is source code that shows you how to nest try and catch blocks:

```
class myMainException extends Exception {}
class mySecondaryException1 extends Exception {}
class mySecondaryException2 extends Exception {}
class mySecondaryException3 extends Exception {}
...
try {
  ...
  throw new myMainException();
  ...
}
catch(myMainException e) {
  ...
  try {
    ...
    if (myCondition)
      throw new mySecondaryException2();
    ...
  }
  catch (mySecondaryException1 e1) {
    ...
  }
  catch (mySecondaryException2 e2) {
    ...
  }
  catch (mySecondaryException3 e3) {
    ...
  }
  ...
}
catch(Throwable t) {
  ...
}
```

This code shows the declaration of the exception classes MainException, mySecondaryException1, mySecondaryException2, and mySecondaryException3. The method main() throws a MainException object inside the outer try block; this block is followed by two catch clauses. Note that the first catch clause handles the MainException exception, whereas the second one handles all other exceptions. The first catch clause contains a nested try and catch block. Be aware that the try block may trigger any of the mySecondaryException1, mySecondaryException2, and mySecondaryException3 exceptions. The inner try block is followed by three catch clauses to handle these three exceptions.

Nested exception handlers handle new exceptions that occur when you are dealing with other exceptions.

Standard Exceptions

Java defines a set of basic exception classes that represent the most common runtime errors. The following table lists these exceptions and indicates their lineage. The hierarchy of Java classes contains other classes to support additional errors and exceptions.

Exception Class	Parent Class	Purpose
Throwable	Object	Parent of exception subhierarchy.
Exception	Throwable	Parent of exception classes.
ClassNotFoundException	Exception	Error in loading a class.
CloseNotSupportedException	Exception	Error in closing an object.
IllegalAccessException	Exception	Error in loading a class.
InterruptedException	Exception	Error generated when a thread is waiting, sleeping, or otherwise paused for a long time and another thread interrupts it by using the interrupt method in the class Thread.
RunTimeException	Exception	Parent of classes that represent more specific types of runtime exceptions.
ArithmeticException	RunTimeException	Arithmetic exception.
ArrayStoreException	RunTimeException	Error due to attempting to store the wrong type of object in an array of objects.
ClassCastException	RunTimeException	Error due to casting an object to the wrong class
IllegalArgumentException	RunTimeException	Error indicates that a method has been passed by an illegal or inappropriate argument.
IllegalThreadStateException	IllegalArgument Exception	Error due to an inappropriate statement for an operation.

Exception Class	Parent Class	Purpose
NumberFormatException	IllegalArgument Exception	Error signals that the application has attempted to convert a string to one of the numeric types but that the string lacks the appropriate format.
IllegalMonitorState Exception	RunTimeException	Error related to a thread operation.
IndexOutOfBounds Exception	RunTimeException	Error generated by an index value (e.g., for an array, string, or vector) being out of range.
ArrayIndexOutOfBounds Exception	IndexOutOfBounds Exception	Error due to the index of an array being out of range.
StringIndexOutOfBounds Exception	IndexOutOfBounds Exception	Error due to the index of a string being out of range.
NegativeArraySizeException	RunTimeException	Error generated by attempting to allocate a negative number of elements to an array.
NullPointerException	RunTimeException	Error due to attempting to use null when an object is required.
SecurityException	RunTimeException	Error thrown by security manager to flag security violation.

Static Attributes

When you create a class instance, that instance has its own copy of the class attributes. This feature allows each instance to maintain its own information separate from other class instances. Sometimes, though, you need attributes to conceptually belong to the class and not to any particular instance. Java supports this feature by offering static attributes and methods. Therefore, while there are as many copies of nonstatic attributes as there are instances, there is only one copy of a static attribute, regardless of the number of class instances. In fact, the static attributes of a class *do* exist and they *are* accessible, even if you have not yet created any instances of that class.

What are static attributes good for? Static attributes essentially serve classes whose instances need to or can (for the sake of saving memory space) share information. The following are several cases where you can use a static attribute in a class:

✦ **Counting the number of class instances.** In this case, the static attribute keeps track of the number of instances. The constructors of the class need to increment the value of the instance counter. To decrement that counter, you need to declare a special method that you call before the object reaches the end of its lifespan.

✦ **Shared information.** The static attributes in a class can support a miniature database that provides common information to the class instances (such as general constants that are shared by all class instances). Therefore, when you use static attributes, you can eliminate redundant information and save space.

✦ **Shared error status.** You can use static attributes to consolidate managing logical errors that occur while invoking methods.

✦ **Instance communication.** The static attributes of a class can support the interaction between two or more class instances.

Java also offers static methods to access nonpublic static attributes. Java does not allow static methods to directly access nonstatic attributes. This is because you can use static methods when there are no class instances — there are no copies of nonstatic attributes in memory. To access nonstatic attributes in a static method, that method needs to create a class instance. The best example is the creation of a class instance in the method main() — the most common static method that you've seen so far!

Static attributes and methods exist regardless of the number of class instances.

The following is an example of a class that has two static members:

```
class myArray {
    protected static int m_nCountInstances = 0;
    protected static String m_ErrorMessage = "";
    protected int m_nArr[];
    ...
    public myArray(int nNumElems) {
        ...
        m_nCountInstances++;
        ...
    }
    ...
    public static void decrInstCount()
    {
        m_nCountInstances-;
    }
    ...
```

```
public static int getNumInstances() {
  return m_nCountInstances;
}

public static String getErrorMessage() {
  return m_ErrorMessage;
}
...
}
```

This code declares the class myArray to support arrays of integers. The class declares the following static attributes:

+ The int-type static attribute m_nCountInstances stores the number of class instances. The class declaration initializes this attribute to 0.

+ The String-type attribute m_ErrorMessage stores the error message for the last error in accessing any class instance.

The class declares a constructor that, among other tasks, increments the value of the static attribute m_nCountInstances. The class also declares the static void method decrInstCount() to decrement the value in the static attribute m_nCountInstances. In addition, the class declares the static methods getNumInstances() and getErrorMessage() to return the values of the static attributes m_nCountInstances and m_ErrorMessage, respectively.

## Part VIII

Strings and Methods

This part covers strings and methods. I cover the role of methods, how to declare them, and how to exit them. I also talk about static methods and how they differ from ordinary methods.

I also cover the class String and its relevant methods that help you manipulate and query characters stored in strings. For example, you will learn how to search for characters, concatenate them, compare strings, copy characters, trim leading and trailing space, and so on.

In this part

- ↙ **Declaring the syntax of a method**
- ↙ **Exiting methods**
- ↙ **Working with methods**
- ↙ **Using static methods**
- ↙ **Using the class** String

Declaring the Syntax of a Method

To declare a method in a Java class, you must use the following general syntax:

```
class className {
  returnType methodName([optionalParameterList])
  {
    declarations and statements
    return aValue;
  }
}
```

This general syntax shows the following components of a method:

◆ The returnType represents the name of a predefined or user-defined data type. If the return type of a method is void, the compiler sees that the method returns nothing — the method returns no data. Methods with the void return type simply perform tasks.

◆ The methodName represents the name of your method. This name should be reasonably short and descriptive of what the method does. For example, if a method adds numbers, you could call it addNumbers or addNums.

◆ The optionalParameterList represents an optional list of parameters that supply the method with data. The method uses this data to perform its task and respond appropriately. This list separates the parameters using commas, regardless of the number of parameters in the method. If the method has no parameters, it uses either empty parentheses or the key word *void* inside the parentheses. The compiler treats both forms the same way.

◆ The opening and closing braces contain the method's declarations and statements. These terms make up the *method body.*

◆ The declarations and statements inside the method body declare variables that are *local* to the method (that is, strictly owned and operated by the method). A local variable is defined within the method only. You can declare a local variable *X* and then a global variable *X,* and they don't mean the same thing — they don't share an address. The local variable essentially is born and dies within the execution of the method. The statements can perform any legal operation, including making calculations, displaying output to the screen, reading input from the keyboard, and even calling other methods.

◆ The return statement exits the method and yields a result. Every method, except void methods, must have at least one return statement. The data type of the resulting value and the returnType part must be the same or at least compatible. See Part 3 for more information about predefined data types. You use a return statement in a void method when you want to support an early exit from that method.

Two examples of methods follow:

```
class Hello {
  void Howdy()
  {
    System.out.println("Hello World!\n");
  }
}
```

The following is a description of each part of the preceding method:

✦ The method has the return type void.

✦ The name of the method is Howdy.

✦ The method has no parameters.

✦ The method declares an output statement.

✦ The method returns no value.

In other words, the preceding code declares the method Howdy(), which has the void return type and no parameters. The body of this method contains a single statement that displays the message Hello World! and emits a new line (due to the \n escape sequence characters). Because the method has the void return type, it contains no return statements.

The following is another example:

```
class Numbers {
  double sqr(double x)
  {
    return x * x;
  }
}
```

The preceding method has the following parts:

✦ The method returns the type double.

✦ The name of the method is sqr.

✦ The method has the parameter double x.

✦ The method has the statement return x * x.

✦ The method returns the squared value of the parameter x.

In other words, the preceding code declares the method sqr().
This method has the double return type and one parameter. The
parameter has the type double and the name x. Note that the
sqr() method uses the value of the parameter in the return
statement. This statement multiplies the value of parameter x by
itself (using the operator *) and returns the result (the squared
value of parameter x). Note that the data type associated with the
parameter x and the method's return type are the same: the
predefined data type double. You can use this method in your
own source code to calculate the squared values of floating-point
numbers. The method sqr() can be part of a set of other methods
that you collect or write to support different mathematical
calculations.

When you use or invoke (or, as programmers say, *call*) a method
— that is, tell the method to execute its statements and perform
its task — the most common and appropriate way to pass information to the method is by using the method's *parameters*.

The general syntax for the parameter list that appears in the
method declaration is as follows:

```
dataType1 parameter1, dataType2 parameter2, ...
```

Note that you must define the type and name of each parameter
separately. The name of a parameter must obey the naming rules.
Java does not allow you to group parameters that have the same
data types. Instead, the language syntax requires you to declare
each parameter with its own data type.

The following is an example of a method with a parameter:

```
class Numbers {
  int showAndGetNextInt(int Number)
  {
    // increase value of parameter by 1
    Number = Number + 1;
    System.out.println(Number);
    return Number;
  }
}
```

The method showAndGetNextInt() has a single int-type
parameter Number. The method increases the value of this
parameter, displays its new value, and then returns that new value.

Exiting Methods

Java allows you to use one or more return statements to exit a
method. If the method returns a type other than void, the return

statement needs to return a value. Otherwise, a simple `return` statement does the job.

The following is an example of exiting a method that has a non-`void` type:

```
int getCode(char Letter)
{
  switch (Letter) {
    case 'a':
      return 1;

    case 'b':
      return 2;

    case 'c':
      return 3;

    default:
      return -1;
  }
}
```

This example shows the method `getCode()`, which returns an integer based on the argument for the `char`-type parameter `Letter`. The method uses a `switch` statement to examine the value of the parameter `Letter`. Each `case` label is followed by a `return` statement. This method shows how you can use multiple return statements.

The following is an example of exiting a method that has a `void` type:

```
void showCode(char Letter)
{
  switch (Letter) {
    case 'a':
      displayCode('a');
      return;

    case 'b':
      displayCode('b');
      return;

    case 'c':
      displayCode('c');
      return;

    default:
      return;
  }
}
```

This example shows the method `showCode()`, which displays some numerical code based on the argument for the `char`-type parameter `Letter`. The method uses a `switch` statement to

examine the value of the parameter Letter. Each case label
invokes the method displayCode() and is followed by a simple
return statement.

Messages

A message is the invocation (or call) or a method that is associated with a class instance (that is, an object). Some Java books use
the term *calling a method*. However, this terminology is a hand-me-
down from the days of structured programming. Object-oriented
programming fosters the notion of communicating with objects
using messages. When you send an object a message, that object
uses the proper method in its class to respond to the message.
Messages can have arguments that match the parameters of
the corresponding methods. The general syntax for sending a
message is

```
object.message(agumentlist)
```

Here is an example for sending a message to an object:

```
class myInt {
  protected int m_nInt;

  public void setInt(int nInt)
  {
    m_nInt = nInt;
  }

  public int getInt()
  {
    return m_nInt;
  }

  public static void main(String[] args)
  {
    myInt intObj = new myInt;

    intObj.setInt(10);
    System.out.println("Integer = " +
                        intObj.getInt());
  }
}
```

The preceding example declares the class myInt. This class has
the protected int-type attribute m_nInt and the following
methods:

✦ The method setInt() has the int-type parameter nInt and
   assigns the value of that parameter to the attribute m_nInt.

✦ The method getInt returns the value of the attribute
   m_nInt.

✦ The static method `main()` declares the local object `intObj` as an instance of class `myInt`. This method assigns the integer 10 to that object by sending the message `setInt()` to the object. The argument for this message is the integer 10. The object responds by executing the code for the method `setInt()`. The method then displays the value in object `intObj` by sending the message `getInt()` to that object. The object responds by executing the code for the method `getInt()`.

Methods

A method is part of a class that supports a class operation. Java methods are similar to functions and member functions in other programming languages like Basic, C, and C++. A class contains a set of methods to support its operations. Methods may initialize attributes, set new values to these attributes, query the value of these attributes, perform calculations, display windows, respond to events, draw graphics, and so on. A method is the smallest unit of executable code. In a sense, methods breathe life into classes and therefore into programs. See the section "Declaring the Syntax of a Method" to find out more about declaring methods. Also see the section "Messages" to find out more about invoking methods with objects.

Static Methods

Static methods are special methods that work with static attributes. Conceptually, static methods differ from nonstatic methods by being regarded as owned by the class itself and not associated with any class instance. You can invoke a static method even when there are no class instances because static methods work with static members. The latter exist regardless of the number of class instances. By contrast, to invoke a nonstatic method, you must have a class instance. For more information on how static methods and attributes work together, see "Static Attributes" in Part VII.

To declare a method as static, simply insert the reserved word `static` before the method's return type.

The following is an example of a class that has three static methods:

```
class myArray {
  protected static int m_nCountInstances = 0;
  protected static String m_ErrorMessage = "";
  protected int m_nArr[];
  ...
  public myArray(int nNumElems) {
    ...
    m_nCountInstances++;
    ...
  }
  ...
  public static void decrInstCount()
  {
    m_nCountInstances-;
  }
  ...
  public static int getNumInstances() {
    return m_nCountInstances;
  }

  public static String getErrorMessage() {
    return m_ErrorMessage;
  }
  ...
  public static void main(String[] args)
  {
    System.out.println("There are " +
        myArray.getNumInstances() + " instances");
    {
      myArray arrObj1 = new myArray(10);
      myArray arrObj2 = new myArray(20);
      System.out.println("There are " +
          myArray.getNumInstances() + " instances");
      myArray.decrInstCount();
      myArray.decrInstCount();
    }
    System.out.println("There are " +
        myArray.getNumInstances() + " instances");
  }
}
```

This code declares the class myArray to support arrays of
integers. The class declares the following static attributes:

> ◆ The int-type static attribute m_nCountInstances stores the
> number of class instances. The class declaration initializes
> this attribute to 0.

> ◆ The String-type attribute m_ErrorMessage stores the error
> message for the last error in accessing any class instance.

The class declares a constructor that, among other tasks, increments the value of the static attribute m_nCountInstances. The
class also declares the static void method decrInstCount() to
decrement the value in the static attribute

m_nCountInstances. In addition, the class declares the static
methods getNumInstances() and getErrorMessage() to
return the values of the static attributes m_nCountInstances
and m_ErrorMessage, respectively. The static method main
performs the following tasks:

+ Displays the initial number of class instances by sending the
  message getNumInstances() to the class myArray itself (at
  this point there are no instances of class myArray).

+ Declares the objects arrObj1 and arrObj2 as instances of
  class myArray in a nested block.

+ Displays the current number of class instances by sending the
  message getNumInstances() to the class myArray itself.
  You can use either object instead of the class name.

+ Decreases the instance counts by sending the message
  decrInstCount() to the class myArray. Again, you can use
  either object instead of the class name.

+ Repeats the preceding task before reaching the end of the
  nested block.

+ Displays the current number of class instances by sending the
  message getNumInstances() to the class myArray itself (at
  this point there are no instances of class myArray).

Strings

Although Java does not support a predefined data type for strings,
it uses the class String, which is part of the java.lang library.
This class supports the following general categories of operations:

+ Creating string objects.

+ Copying and concatenating strings.

+ Accessing characters in a string.

+ Extracting substrings.

+ Manipulating the characters in a string. This set of operations
  includes trimming leading and trailing spaces, converting
  characters to uppercase, and converting characters to
  lowercase.

+ Comparing strings.

+ Searching for substrings. This kind of operation includes
  searching for substrings at the beginning and end of a string.

+ Converting from the predefined types to strings.

The following is the declaration of the class String:

```
public final class java.lang.String
    extends java.lang.Object
{
    // Constructors
    public String();
    public String(byte ascii[], int hibyte);
    public String(byte ascii[], int hibyte,
                            int offset, int count);
        public String(char value[]);
    public String(char value[], int offset,
                    int count);

    public String(String value);
    public String(StringBuffer buffer);

    // Methods
    public char charAt(int index);
    public int compareTo(String anotherString);
    public String concat(String str);
    public static String copyValueOf(char data[]);

        public static String copyValueOf(char
    data[],
        int offset, int count);
    public boolean endsWith(String suffix);
    public boolean equals(Object anObject);
    public boolean equalsIgnoreCase(
        String anotherString);
    public void getBytes(int srcBegin, int srcEnd,
        byte dst[], int dstBegin);
    public void getChars(int srcBegin, int srcEnd,
        char dst[], int dstBegin);
    public int hashCode();
    public int indexOf(int ch);
    public int indexOf(int ch, int fromIndex);
    public int indexOf(String str);
    public int indexOf(String str, int fromIndex);
    public String intern();
    public int lastIndexOf(int ch);
    public int lastIndexOf(int ch, int fromIndex);
    public int lastIndexOf(String str);
    public int lastIndexOf(String str, int
    fromIndex);
    public int length();
    public boolean regionMatches(boolean
    ignoreCase,
        int toffset, String other, int ooffset,
        int len);
        public boolean regionMatches(int toffset,
        String other, int ooffset, int len);
    public String replace(char oldChar, char
    newChar);
    public boolean startsWith(String prefix);
    public boolean startsWith(String prefix,
        int toffset);
```

```
public String substring(int beginIndex);
public String substring(int beginIndex,
    int endIndex);
public char[] toCharArray();
public String toLowerCase();
public String toString();
public String toUpperCase();
public String trim();
public static String valueOf(boolean b);
public static String valueOf(char c);
public static String valueOf(char data[]);
public static String valueOf(char data[],
    int offset, int count);
public static String valueOf(double d);
public static String valueOf(float f);
public static String valueOf(int i);
public static String valueOf(long l);
public static String valueOf(Object obj);
}
```

The first character in a `String` instance has the index of 0. Attempting to access a character that does not exist causes a runtime error.

The valid character indices of a string range from 0 to the number of characters in that string minus one.

Extracting characters from a string

Many string-manipulation operations involve extracting substrings from strings to examine the characters in these substrings. The class `String` offers the following two versions of the method `substring()` to extract substrings from a string:

```
public String substring(int beginIndex);
public String substring(int beginIndex,
    int endIndex);
```

The first version extracts a substring from the index that is specified by the parameter `beginIndex` to the end of the string. The second version extracts a substring from the characters that are specified by parameters `beginIndex` and `endIndex`. The latter parameter is the index of the first character that is *not* included in the extracted substring.

The method `substring()` is not very forgiving of bad arguments for the parameters `beginIndex` and `endIndex`. Therefore, make sure that you verify the arguments for these parameters before you include them in a `substring()` message. The valid arguments for the parameter `beginIndex` are from 0 to the index of the last character (that is, the number of characters minus 1). The valid arguments for the parameter `endIndex` are in the range of 1 to the index just beyond the last character (that is, the number of characters). Make a note of these values.

The following is an example that shows you how the two versions
of the method `substring()` work:

```
String Str = new String("Java");
// next statement displays: ava
System.out.println(Str.substring(1));
// next statement displays: av
System.out.println(Str.substring(1, 2));
```

This example declares the string `Str` and initializes it with the
word *Java*. The first output statement displays the substring of
`Str` that starts with the second character. This statement sends
the message `substring()` to the object `Str`. The argument for
this message is the index 1. The statement displays the text *ava*.
Then the second output statement displays the substring of `Str`
that includes the second and third characters. This statement
sends the message `substring()` to the object `Str`. The arguments for this message are the indices 1 and 2. The statement
displays the text *av*.

Manipulating characters in strings

You often need to convert the characters in a string to uppercase
or lowercase. You may also need to remove the leading and trailing
spaces in a string to examine the more relevant characters. The
class `String` offers the following methods to trim and change the
case of characters in strings:

✦ The method `trim()` returns a string after removing the
   leading and trailing white-space characters from the source
   string.

✦ The method `toUpperCase()` returns a string with uppercase
   characters.

✦ The method `toLowerCase()` returns a string with lowercase
   characters.

Note that none of these methods has parameters.

The methods `trim()`, `toUpperCase()`, and `toLowerCase()` do
not automatically store the altered characters in the source string.
To do that, you must assign the result of the methods back to the
source string.

The following is an example that shows you how to use the
methods `trim()`, `toUpperCase()`, and `toLowerCase()`:

```
String Str = new String("  Java   ");
Str = Str.trim();
// next statement displays: Java
System.out.println(Str);
// next statement displays: JAVA
```

```
System.out.println(Str.toUpperCase());
// next statement displays: java
System.out.println(Str.toLowerCase());
```

This example declares the string `Str` and initializes it with the string literal `"   Java   "`. The first statement trims the leading and trailing spaces in the object `Str` and assigns the result back to that object. Note that the statement sends the message `trim()` to the object `Str`. The first output statement displays the characters in `Str`, which are `"Java"`. Then the second output statement displays the uppercase characters of the string in `Str` by sending the message `toUpperCase()` to that string. The last output statement displays the lowercase characters of the string in `Str` by sending the message `toLowerCase()` to that string.

Comparing strings

Java allows you to use the relational operators with the instances of the class `String`. In addition, the class `String` offers the following methods to compare strings:

✦ The `int`-type method `compareTo(String anotherString)` compares the string that is receiving the message `compareTo()` (referred to in this text as *this string*) with the string that is the argument for the parameter `anotherString` (referred to here as *the argument string*). The method returns an integer that reflects how the two strings compare. Note that the result is 0 if the argument string is equal to this string. The result is less than 0 if this string is lexicographically less than the string argument. Finally, the result is greater than 0 if this string is lexicographically greater than the string argument.

✦ The `boolean`-type method `equals(Object anObject)` compares the string that is receiving the message `equals()` with the string that is the argument for the parameter `anObject`. If the two strings are equal, the method yields `true`. Otherwise, the method returns `false`. The comparison is case sensitive — the method distinguishes between upper-case and lowercase characters.

✦ The `boolean`-type method `equalsIgnoreCase(String anotherString)` compares the string that is receiving the message `equalsIgnoreCase()` with the string that is the argument for the parameter `anotherString`. If the two strings are equal (regardless of differences in case), the method yields `true`. Otherwise, the method returns `false`.

The following is an example of using the method `compareTo()`:

```
String Str1 = new String("Java");
String Str2 = new String("JAVA");
int nRes = Str1.compareTo(Str2);
System.out.println("String comparison code = " +
   nRes);
```

This example declares and initializes the strings `Str1` and `Str2` with the string literals `"Java"` and `"JAVA"`, respectively. The example compares the two strings by sending the message `compareTo()` to the object `Str1`. Note that the argument for this message is the string `Str2`. The output statement displays the result, which is less than 0 because the string `"JAVA"` is lexicographically less than the string `"Java"`.

The following example uses the methods `equals()` and `equalsIgnoreCase()`:

```
String Str1 = new String("Java");
String Str2 = new String("JAVA");
if (Str1.equals(Str2))
   System.out.println("Strings are equal!");
if (Str1.equalsIgnorecase(Str2))
   System.out.println("Strings are equal " +
      "(case insensitive)!");
```

This example declares and initializes the strings `Str1` and `Str2` with the string literals `"Java"` and `"JAVA"`, respectively. Note that the example has two `if` statements. The first `if` statement performs a case-sensitive comparison between the strings `Str1` and `Str2`. The tested condition sends the message `equals()` to the string `Str1`. The argument for this message is string `Str2`. Because the characters in strings `Str1` and `Str2` are not the same, the tested condition is `false`. Then the second `if` statement performs a case-insensitive comparison between the strings `Str1` and `Str2`. The tested condition sends the message `equalsIgnoreCase()` to the string `Str1`. Note that the argument for this message is string `Str2`. Because the characters in strings `Str1` and `Str2` are the same regardless of case, the tested condition is `true`.

Searching in strings

Searching for characters and substrings in strings is one of the most common text-processing operations. These searches either serve to locate and display text or to find and replace text. The class `String` offers the search-related methods `indexOf()`, `lastIndexOf()`, `startsWith()`, and `endsWith()`.

The method indexOf( )

The class String provides three versions of the method
indexOf( ); these versions search forward in a string (that is,
starting from the leading to the trailing characters). The following
are the declarations of the methods indexOf( ):

```
public int indexOf(int ch);
public int indexOf(int ch, int fromIndex);
public int indexOf(String str);
public int indexOf(String str, int fromIndex);
```

An explanation of the versions is as follows:

✦ The first version of method indexOf( ) searches for the first
occurrence of the search character (represented by the int-
type parameter ch).

✦ The second version of method indexOf( ) searches for the
first occurrence of the search character (represented by the
int-type parameter ch), starting at the character index
fromIndex.

✦ The third version of method indexOf( ) searches for the first
occurrence of the search string (represented by the String-
type parameter str).

✦ The last version of method indexOf( ) searches for the first
occurrence of the search string (represented by the String-
type parameter str), starting at the character index
fromIndex.

Each version of the method indexOf( ) returns the index of the
matching character or yields –1 if no match is found.

The following is an example of using the method indexOf( ):

```
String Str = new String("01234567890123456789");
System.out.println(Str.indexOf('3'));
System.out.println(Str.indexOf('0', 2));
System.out.println(Str.indexOf("123"));
System.out.println(Str.indexOf("123", 7));
```

This example declares the string Str and initializes it with the
string literal "01234567890123456789". The example then uses
the following four output statements to test the various versions
of the method indexOf( ):

✦ The first output statement uses the method indexOf(int) to
search for the last occurrence of the character 3 in string Str.
The message Str.indexOf('3') returns 13.

◆ The second output statement uses the method
indexOf(int, int) to search for the last occurrence of the
character 0, after the third character, in the string Str. The
message Str.indexOf('0', 2) returns 11.

◆ The third output statement uses the method
indexOf(String) to search for the last occurrence of the
substring "123" in string Str. The message
Str.indexOf("123") returns 11.

◆ The last output statement uses the method
indexOf(String, int) to search for the last occurrence of
the substring "123", after the eighth character, in string Str.
The message Str.indexOf("123", 7) returns 11.

The method lastIndexOf ( )

The class String offers four versions of the method
lastIndexOf(); these versions search backward in a string (that
is, starting from the trailing to the leading characters). The
following are the declarations of the methods lastIndexOf():

```
public int lastIndexOf(int ch, int fromIndex);
public int lastIndexOf(String str);
public int lastIndexOf(String str, int fromIndex);
```

The parameters of the these methods are similar to those of the
method indexOf(). Each version of method lastIndexOf()
returns the index of the matching character or yields –1 if no
match is found.

The following is an example of using the method lastIndexOf():

```
String Str = new String("01234567890123456789");
System.out.println(Str.lastIndexOf('3'));
System.out.println(Str.lastIndexOf('0', 2));
System.out.println(Str.lastIndexOf("123"));
System.out.println(Str.lastIndexOf("123", 7));
```

This example declares the string Str and initializes it with the
string literal "01234567890123456789". The example then uses
four output statements to test the various versions of the method
lastIndexOf():

◆ The first output statement uses the method
lastIndexOf(int) to search for the first occurrence of the
character 3 in the string Str. The message
Str.lastIndexOf('3') returns 4.

◆ The second output statement uses the method
lastIndexOf(int, int) to search for the first occurrence
of the character 0, after the third character, in the string Str.
The message Str.lastIndexOf('0', 2) returns 11.

◆ The third output statement uses the method
lastIndexOf(String) to search for the first occurrence of
the substring "123" in the string Str. The message
Str.lastIndexOf("123") returns 2.

◆ The last output statement uses the method
lastIndexOf(String, int) to search for the first occurrence of the substring "123", after the eighth character, in
string Str. The message Str.lastIndexOf("123", 7)
returns 12.

The method startsWith ( )

The class String offers the logical method startsWith(), which
allows you to search for prefix characters in a string. The two
versions of this method are as follows:

```
public boolean startsWith(String prefix);
public boolean startsWith(String prefix, int
    toffset);
```

The following is an example of using the method startsWith():

```
String Str = new String("01234567890123456789");
System.out.println(Str.startsWith("0123"));
System.out.println(Str.startsWith("0123", 10));
```

This example declares the string Str and initializes it with the
string literal "01234567890123456789". The example then uses
two output statements to test the various versions of the method
startsWith():

◆ The first output statement uses the method
startsWith(String) to search for the prefix characters
"0123" in the string Str. The message
Str.startsWith("0123") returns true.

◆ The second output statement uses the method
startsWith(String, int) to search for the prefix characters "0123", at the eleventh character, in string Str. The
message Str.startsWith("0123", 10) returns true.

The method endsWith ( )

The class String offers the method endsWith() to determine
whether a string ends with the characters specified by a substring.
The declaration of the method endsWith() is

```
public boolean endsWith(String suffix);
```

The method `endsWith()` returns `true` if the character sequence that is represented by the `String`-type parameter `suffix` is the suffix of the character sequence represented by the string that is receiving the message `endsWith()`. Otherwise, the method yields `false`.

The following is an example of using the method `endsWith()`:

```
String Str = new String("01234567890123456789");
System.out.println(Str.endsWith("789"));
System.out.println(Str.endsWith("012"));
```

This example declares the string `Str` and initializes it with the string literal `"01234567890123456789"`. The example then uses two output statements to test the various versions of the method `endsWith()`:

✦ The first output statement searches for the suffix `"789"` in the string `Str`. Because that string ends with the characters `"789"`, the Boolean message `endsWith()` yields `true`.

✦ The second output statement searches for the suffix `"012"` in the string `Str`. Because that string does not end with the characters `"012"`, the Boolean message `endsWith()` yields `false`.

Converting between strings and other types

Converting between strings and other types (mostly integers and floating-point numbers) is a task that is common to reading and writing text files that store numbers as strings. The `String` class (as well as the classes `Boolean`, `Integer`, `Character`, `Long`, `Double`, and `Float`) uses the static method `valueOf()` to convert between strings and other types. Furthermore, the class `String` offers multiple versions of method `valueOf()` to convert the values from predefined data types into strings. The following are the declarations of these versions of the method `valueOf()`:

```
public static String valueOf(boolean b);
public static String valueOf(char c);
public static String valueOf(double d);
public static String valueOf(float f);
public static String valueOf(int i);
public static String valueOf(long l);
```

The following is an example of using the versions of the method `valueOf()`:

```
// display the string 'true'
boolean ok = true;
System.out.println("'" + String.valueOf(ok) + "'");
// display the string 'A'
char Letter = 'A';
```

```
System.out.println("'" + String.valueOf(Letter) +
    "'");
// display the string '3.14'
double Rate = 3.14;
System.out.println("'" + String.valueOf(Rate) +
    "'");
// display the string '1000'
int Num = 1000;
System.out.println("'" + String.valueOf(Num) +
    "'");
```

This example contains the declarations of diverse variables and output statements that display the contents of these variables by using the method `String.valueOf()`. The example contains the following declarations and output:

✦ The `boolean`-type variable `ok` initialized with the value `true`. The first output statements display the string `'true'` by using the method `String.valueOf()` with the argument `ok`.

✦ The `char`-type variable `Letter` initialized with the characters `'A'`. The second output statements display the string `'A'` by using the method `String.valueOf()` with the argument `Letter`.

✦ The `double`-type variable `Rate` initialized with the value `3.14`. The third output statements display the string `'3.14'` by using the method `String.valueOf()` with the argument `Rate`.

✦ The `int`-type variable `Num` initialized with the value `1000`. The last output statements display the string `'1000'` by using the method `String.valueOf()` with the argument `Num`.

When converting from a string to a predefined type, you must use the classes `Boolean`, `Integer`, `Character`, `Long`, `Double`, or `Float` as intermediaries. The following is an example:

```
String Str = new String("1234");
Integer IntObj = new Integer(0);
IntObj = Integer.valueOf(Str);
// display 1234
System.out.println(IntObj);
```

This example declares the string `Str` and initializes it with the string literal `"1234"`. The example also declares the object `IntObj` as an instance of the class `Integer`. This code then converts the string in object `Str` into an integer by using the method `Integer.valueOf()` and the argument `Str`. The output statements display the integer 1234, which is stored in the object `IntObj`.

The following is another example:

```
String Str = new String("12.34");
Double DblObj = new Double(0);
DblObj = Double.valueOf(Str);
// display 12.34
System.out.println(IntObj);
```

This example declares the string `Str` and initializes it with the string literal `"12.34"`. The example also declares the object `DblObj` as an instance of the class `Double`. This code then converts the string in object `Str` into a floating-point number by using the method `Double.valueOf()` and the argument `Str`. The output statements display the floating-point number 12.34, which is stored in the object `DblObj`.

Using the String constructors

The class `String` offers seven constructors to give you different ways to create an instance. I focus on the following class constructors:

◆ The parameterless constructor creates an empty string.

◆ The constructor `String(byte ascii[], int hibyte)` creates a string using the array of ASCII codes (that is, the standard numeric codes for the various characters) `ascii[]` and the `int`-type mask `hibyte`.

◆ The constructor `String(byte ascii[], int hibyte, int offset, int count)` creates a string using `count` elements in the array of ASCII codes `ascii[]` and the `int`-type mask `hibyte`. The `int`-type parameter `offset` specifies the index of the first array element to supply the instance with data.

◆ The constructor `String(char value[])` creates a string using the array of characters `value[]`.

◆ The constructor `String(char value[], int offset, int count)` creates a string using `count` characters in the array of characters `value[]`.The `int`-type parameter offset specifies the index of the first array element to supply the instance with data.

◆ The constructor `String(String value)` creates a string using the characters in the existing string `value`.

The following is an example of creating class instances using these constructors:

```
byte byteArr[] = { 97, 97, 97, 97, 97 };
char charArr[] = { 'J', 'a', 'v', 'a' };
```

```
String String1 = new String();
String String2 = new String(byteArr, 0);
String String3 = new String(byteArr, 0, 1, 2);
String String4 = new String(charArr);
String String5 = new String(charArr, 1, 3);
String String6 = new String(String4);
```

This example declares and initializes the byte-type array byteArr and the char-type array charArr. The example also declares the instances String1 through String6 of the class String.

The instances are described as follows:

✦ The example declares the instance String1 using the parameterless constructor. This instance initially stores an empty string.

✦ The code declares the instance String2 using the constructor String(byte ascii[], int hibyte). The declaration creates an instance that stores the string "aaaaa" because the constructor uses the byte-type array byteArr. This array stores five characters, which are all the lowercase letter *a*.

✦ The example declares the instance String3 using the constructor String(byte ascii[], int hibyte, int offset, int count). This declaration creates an instance that stores the string "aaa". The constructor copies three characters from array byteArr, starting at the second element.

✦ The code declares the instance String4 using the constructor String(char value[]). This declaration creates an instance that stores the string "Java" because the constructor uses the char-type array charArr. This array stores the characters *J, a, v,* and *a*.

✦ The example declares the instance String5 using the constructor String(char value[], int offset, int count). This declaration creates an instance that stores the string "ava" because the constructor uses the char-type array charArr and copies three characters starting with the second element.

✦ The code declares the instance String6 using the constructor String(String). This declaration creates an instance that stores the string "Java" because the constructor uses the instance String4 as a source for characters.

Obtaining the length of a string

Many string-manipulation operations require you to know the current number of characters in a string. The class String offers the method length() to return the number of characters in a string.

The following is an example of using the method length():

```
String StrObj = new String("Java");
System.out.println("String contains " +
    StrObj.length() + " characters");
```

This example creates the class instance StrObj and initializes it with the string "Java". The output statement displays the number of characters (which is four) in the instance StrObj. This statement obtains that number by sending the message length() to the object StrObj.

Remember that the number of characters in a string is one higher than the index of the last character in that string.

Copying characters

You can copy characters to a string by using the following options:

✦ Use the assignment operator to copy the characters of an instance of the class String to another.

✦ Copy the characters to an array of characters that act as a buffer and then copy the characters from that array to another string. The method toCharArray() copies the characters of a String instance to an array of characters. The static method copyValueOf() copies the characters of an array to a String instance. Use this method when you want to alter the characters in the array before you copy it back to the original string or to another string.

The following is an example of using these two methods to copy characters:

```
String Str1 = new String("Java");
String Str2 = new String();
String Str3 = new String();
char charArr[] = new char[Str1.length()];
// use the assignment operator
Str2 = Str3
// use the methods that work with the array of
    characters
// copy from Str1 to the array
charArr = Str1.toCharArray();
// copy from the array to the string Str3
Str3 = String.copyValueOf(charArr);
```

This example creates the objects Str1, Str2, and Str3, which are instances of the class String. The declaration initializes the object Str1 with the string "Java". The code also declares the char-type array charArr and sets its number of elements equal to the number of characters in the object Str1.

The example copies the characters in the string Str1 to the string Str2 using the assignment operator. This is a direct and simple way to copy the characters between two strings. By contrast, the example copies the characters in the string Str1 to the string Str2 using the methods toCharArray() and copyValueOf() and the array charArr. This method is a two-step operation that involves an intermediate buffer. The next programming example shows you how this method becomes worthwhile.

Accessing characters

The class String offers the method charAt(int index) to recall a character at a specified index. The index 0 accesses the first character. Can you store a character at a specific index? Unfortunately, the class String offers no method to store a character at a specific index. Consequently, you need to copy the string's characters to an array of characters, manipulate the characters in that array, and then copy the array's characters back to the string. It's definitely awkward!

The following is an example of recalling characters from a string using the method charAt():

```
String Str1 = new String("Java");
char charArr[] = new char[Str1.length()];
for (int i = 0; i < Str1.length(); i++)
  charArr[i] = Str1.charAt(i);
```

This example creates the object Str1 and initializes it with the string "Java". The code also declares the char-type array charArr and sets its number of elements equal to the number of characters in the object Str1. The example uses a for loop to copy the characters of the string Str1 to the array charArr. Each loop iteration copies the character at the index i (the variable *i* is the loop control variable). Then the loop statement obtains the character from the string by sending the message charAt() to the object Str1. The argument for this message is the loop control variable.

Concatenating strings

Java allows you to concatenate strings by using the operator + or by using the method concat() in the class String. The method concat() concatenates the argument of the message and the target of the message; it also returns the concatenated string.

The following is an example of using the method concat():

```
String Str1 = new String("Java");
String Str2 = new String(" is cool!");
String Str3 = new String();
// concatenate strings Str1 and Str2
// store result in Str3
Str3 = Str3.concat(Str1);
Str3 = Str3.concat(Str2);
// concatenate strings Str1 and Str2
// store result in Str1
Str1 = Str1.concat(Str2);
```

This example declares the three String-type objects Str1, Str2, and Str3. It also assigns the strings "Java" and " is cool!" to the strings Str1 and Str2. The example then performs the following tasks:

✦ Concatenates the string Str1 to Str3 by sending the message concat() to the object Str3. The argument for this message is the object Str1. The string Str3 now contains "Java".

✦ Concatenates the string Str2 to Str3 by sending the message concat() to the object Str3. The argument for this message is the object Str2. The string Str3 now contains "Java is cool!".

✦ Concatenates the string Str2 to Str1 by sending the message concat() to the object Str1. The argument for this message is the object Str2. The string Str1 now contains "Java is cool!".

Handling the Mouse and Keyboard

This part looks at handling the use of the keyboard and mouse. The text covers the methods that allow you to intercept keystrokes from the user and respond to them. As for the mouse, this part shows you how to detect mouse clicks and to track the movements of the mouse.

In this part

↙ **Managing keyboard input**

↙ **Handling mouse clicks**

↙ **Managing mouse movements**

Events

The Java AWT allows you to respond to events using various methods. This section focuses on the methods `handleEvent()` and `action()`.

The method handleEvent ( )

The class `Container` declares the method `handleEvent()`, which is declared as follows:

```
public boolean handleEvent(Event evt)
{
  // statements to handle events
  return booleanExpression;
}
```

The parameter `evt` is an object that describes the event. Note that the method responds to any event that occurs within a component. The method `handleEvent()` yields `true` to signal that it has successfully dealt with the action. Otherwise, the method returns `false` when the event that triggered the action should be passed up to the component's parent.

A typical way to use the parameter `evt` is to access its public attribute `target`. You compare this attribute with the name of a control class. The following is an example:

```
public boolean handleEvent(Event evt)
  {
    if (evt.target instanceof Scrollbar) {
      // statements to handle event
    }
    return true;
  }
```

This example uses an `if` statement to determine whether the event was generated by a scrollbar component. The `if` statement uses the `instanceof` operator to make this determination.

The method action ( )

The method `action()` responds to an action that occurs inside this component. The general syntax for the method is as follows:

```
public boolean action(Event evt, Object arg)
  {
    // statements to handle events
    return booleanExpression;
  }
```

The parameter evt is the event that produced the action, and the parameter arg is the action itself. This method is usually called by the method handleEvent(), in which case the parameter arg contains additional information related to the event. The specific value and type of the parameter arg depend on the component that originally triggered the action.

The method action() yields true to signal that it successfully dealt with the action. The method yields false when the event that triggered the action should be passed up to the component's parent. Most applications should return either true or the value of the expression super.handleEvent(evt).

The following is an example of using the method action():

```
public boolean action(Event evt, Object arg)
{
    String caption = (String)arg;
    if (evt.target instanceof Button) {
        // statements to respond to clicking a button
        if (caption.equals("Calculate") {
        // respond to button Calculate
        }
        else if (caption.equals("Store") {
        // respond to button Store
        }
        else if (caption.equals("Exit") {
        // respond to button Exit
        }

    }
    return true;
    }
}
```

The method action() responds to the event that is generated by clicking a button. This method uses an if statement to examine the condition (evt.target instanceof Button) and determine if the event was generated by a button. If this condition is true, the method determines which button generated the event. The nested if statements show that the method action() responds to the buttons Calculate, Save, and Exit. This method uses the local string variable caption as a String cast of the parameter arg to store the caption of the button that generated the button click event.

Keyboard Input

The Java AWT library allows you to manage keyboard input in a way that is similar to clicking the mouse. The library offers the methods keyDown() and keyUp() to handle pressing and releasing a key, respectively.

The syntax for the methods keyDown() and keyUp() is as follows:

```
public boolean keyDown(Event evt, int key) {
    handle pressing a key
    return true;
}

public boolean keyUp(Event evt, int key) {
    handle releasing a key
    return true;
}
```

The parameter evt is the same as that in the method mouseDown() and mouseUp(). Note that the int-type parameter key represents the ASCII code for the key that is pressed or released. The methods keyDown() and keyUp() return true to signal that they have successfully handled the key-related event; otherwise, these methods should return false.

You can use the parameter key in the methods keyDown() and keyUp() to detect special keys, such as Home, End, PgUp, and PgDn. The following table shows the values of the constants in the class Event that correspond to the special function keys. For example, to detect pressing F1, you would write the following code:

```
public boolean keyDown(Event evt, int key) {
    if (key == Event.F1)
        statements to handle F1 function key
    other statements to handle response
    return true;
}
```

Constant in Class Event	Function Key
Event.F1 through Event.F12	F1 through F12
Event.DOWN	Down-arrow
Event.END	End
Event.HOME	Home
Event.LEFT	Left-arrow
Event.RIGHT	Right-arrow
Event.PGDN	PgDn
Event.PGUP	PgUp
Event.UP	Up-arrow

The following is an example that shows you how to work with keyboard input. The test program uses a number-guessing game in which the computer guesses a number (between 1 and 1000) that you select. To guide the computer into guessing the number, the program displays the information on the following keys:

✦ Press PgUp when the current guess is lower than the chosen number.

✦ Press PgDn when the current guess is higher than the chosen number.

✦ Press End when the program has guessed the chosen number.

After the program guesses the number, it ignores keyboard input, forcing you to close the HTML file. The following figure shows a sample session with the keys test program.

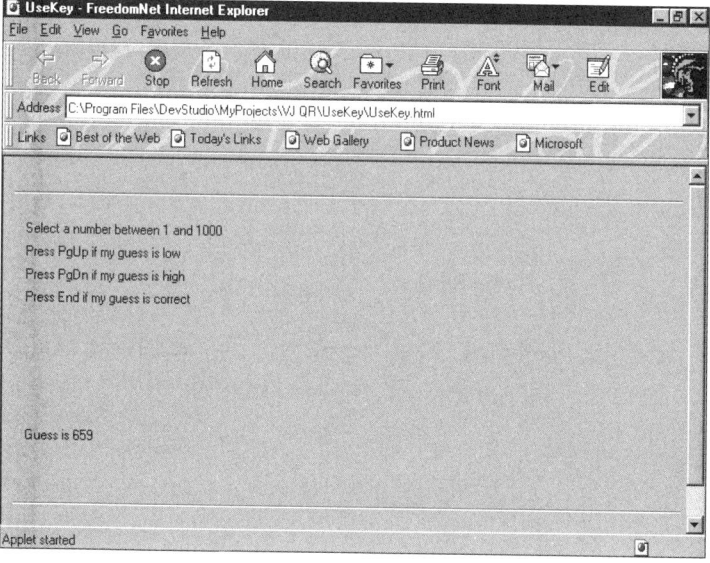

You must first click the mouse button on the drawing area before the program can accept keyboard input.

The following source code defines the keyboard-input program:

```java
import java.applet.*;
import java.awt.*;

public class UseKey extends Applet
{
  protected final int MIN_VAL = 1;
  protected final int MAX_VAL = 1000;
  protected int m_nGuess;
  protected int m_nHi;
  protected int m_nLo;
  protected boolean m_bStop = false;
  protected String m_TopMessage;
  protected String m_BotMessage;
```

(continued)

(continued)

```java
  public String getAppletInfo()
  {
    return "";
  }

  public void init()
  {
    resize(320, 240);

    // set range of current guess
    m_nHi = MAX_VAL;
    m_nLo = MIN_VAL;
    // set initial guess
    m_nGuess = (m_nLo + m_nHi) / 2;
    m_TopMessage = "Select a number between " +
      MIN_VAL + " and " + MAX_VAL;
    m_BotMessage = "Guess is " + m_nGuess;
  }

  public void paint(Graphics g)
  {
    g.drawString(m_TopMessage, 10, 20);
    g.drawString("Press PgUp if my guess is low",
                 10, 40);
    g.drawString("Press PgDn if my guess is high",
                 10, 60);
    g.drawString("Press End if my guess is correct",
                 10, 80);
    g.drawString(m_BotMessage, 10, 200);

  }

  public boolean keyDown(Event evt, int key)
  {
    boolean bUpdate = false;

    // exit if game is over!
    if (m_bStop)
      return true;

    if (key == Event.PGUP) {
      // adjust lower limit of range
      m_nLo = m_nGuess;
      bUpdate = true;
    }
    else if (key == Event.PGDN) {
      // adjust higher limit of range
      m_nHi = m_nGuess;
      bUpdate = true;
    }
    else if (key == Event.END) {
      m_bStop = true;
    }
```

```
      // update guess
      if (bUpdate) {
        // make new guess
        m_nGuess = (m_nLo + m_nHi) / 2;
        // set new guess string
        m_BotMessage = "Guess is " + m_nGuess;
        // update drawing area
        repaint();
      }

      // display last message
      if (m_bStop) {
        m_BotMessage = "I guessed it!";
        repaint();
      }

      return true;
  }
}
```

This code contains the declarations for the attributes and methods of the class UseKey. The class declares the following attributes:

✦ The int-type constants MIN_VAL and MAX_VAL define the range of the number that you choose.

✦ The int-type attribute m_nGuess stores the computer's guess for the number.

✦ The int-type attributes m_nLo and m_nHi store the range for the number. The program updates this range to narrow the search for the number.

✦ The boolean-type attribute m_bStop is a flag that tells the program when to stop reading keyboard input (because it guessed the number).

✦ The String-type attributes m_TopMessage and m_BotMessage display messages about the range of the number and the current guess, respectively.

The next sections show the methods of the class UseKey.

The method init ( )

The method init() performs the following tasks to initialize the drawing area:

✦ Copies the values of constants MAX_VAL and MIN_VAL to the attributes m_nHi and m_nLo, respectively. This task sets the initial range that is used by the program to narrow in on the chosen number.

✦ Calculates the initial guess (as the median of the range defined by the attributes m_nHi and m_nLo) and stores that value in the attribute m_nGuess.

✦ Assigns the top message text to the attribute m_TopMessage. This text specifies the range of the chosen number.

✦ Assigns the bottom message text to the attribute m_BotMessage. This text specifies the initial guess for the number.

The method paint ( )

The method paint() displays text in the drawing area by performing the following tasks:

✦ Displays the text in the attribute m_TopMessage by sending the message drawString() to the Graphics object g. The arguments for this message are the attribute m_TopMessage and the coordinates 10 and 20.

✦ Displays the instructions for using the keyboard by sending a sequence of three drawString() messages to the Graphics object g. The arguments for each message are a string literal (containing the instructions) and the coordinates for displaying that string.

✦ Displays the text in the attribute m_BotMessage by sending the message drawString() to the Graphics object g. The arguments for this message are the attribute m_BotMessage and the coordinates 10 and 200.

The method keyDown ( )

The method keyDown() responds to pressing a key. The method declares the local boolean-type variable bUpdate and performs the following tasks:

✦ Exists when the attribute m_bStop is true. This task uses an if statement that examines the value in that attribute.

✦ Determines whether the parameter key is equal to Event.PGUP (that is, you pressed PgUp). When this condition is true, the method assigns the value of attribute m_nGuess to attribute m_nLo and assigns true to the local variable bUpdate.

✦ Determines whether the parameter key is equal to Event.PGDN (that is, you pressed PgDn). When this condition is true, the method assigns the value of attribute m_nGuess to attribute m_nHi and assigns true to the local variable bUpdate.

+ Determines whether the parameter key is equal to
Event.END (that is, you pressed End). When this condition is
true, the method assigns true to the attribute m_bStop.

+ Determines whether the local variable bUpdate is true. If so,
the method calculates a new guess (and stores it in the
variable m_nGuess), updates the text for the attribute
m_BotMessage, and repaints the drawing area.

+ Determines whether the attribute m_bStop is true. If so, the
method updates the text for the attribute m_BotMessage and
repaints the drawing area.

+ Returns true.

Managing Mouse Clicks

Clicking the mouse is an important part of the graphical user
interface. When you click a mouse button, two things happen: You
press the mouse button down, and then you release it. This action
translates into two events: the mouse-down and mouse-up events.
The AWT library supports the boolean methods mouseDown()
and mouseUp() to handle the mouse-down and mouse-up events,
respectively. The general syntax for these methods is as follows:

```
public boolean mouseDown(Event evt, int x, int y)
{
    statements to handle pressing a mouse button down
    return true;
}

public boolean mouseUp(Event evt, int x, int y)
{
    statements to handle releasing a mouse button
    return true;
}
```

The Event-type parameter evt is an object (discussed next) that
describes the event. The parameters x and y are the coordinates
specifying where the mouse-button event occurs. The methods
mouseDown() and mouseUp() return true to indicate that they
have successfully dealt with the event. Otherwise, the methods
should return false. As a new Java programmer, stay with
returning true for now.

The class Event offers methods that tell you whether Shift and
Ctrl are pressed when you click the mouse. If you're using the
mouse in an advanced way, you need to know this information.
The following boolean methods return the state of Shift and Ctrl:

✦ The method `controlDown()` yields `true` if Ctrl is pressed when the mouse-button event occurs; otherwise, the method returns `false`.

✦ The method `shiftDown()` yields `true` if Shift is pressed when the mouse-button event occurs; otherwise, the method returns `false`.

It's worth pointing out that the Java Applet Wizard can include shell source code for the mouse events, if you select the wizard's options to generate that code.

What about determining whether you clicked the left or right mouse button? The class `Event` has the attribute `modifiers`, which stores information about modifier keys (such as Ctrl and Shift) and about which mouse button you clicked. To determine whether you clicked the right mouse button, perform a bitwise AND operation (using the operator &) on the `modifiers` attribute of the `Event`-type parameter and the constant `Event.META_MASK`. If the result of the operator & is positive, the right mouse button was clicked; otherwise, the left mouse button was clicked. The following is a general form for this query:

```
public boolean mouseDown(Event evt, int x, int y)
{
  if ((evt.modifiers & Event.META_MASK) > 0)
    handle right mouse button
  else
    handle left mouse button
  other statements to handle pressing a mouse
    button down
  return true;
}
```

The methods `mouseDown()` and `mouseUp()` cannot be used interchangeably. The program offers a somewhat different response when using either method. The following test program detects clicking the left and right mouse buttons. When you click either button, the program displays a message telling you which button you clicked and the coordinates where the mouse click occurred.

```
import java.applet.*;
import java.awt.*;
import MouseClicksFrame;

public class MouseClicks extends Applet
{
boolean m_fStandAlone = false;
  protected String m_Message = new
          String("Click a mouse button");

public static void main(String args[])
  {
```

```
    MouseClicksFrame frame = new
        MouseClicksFrame("MouseClicks");

    frame.show();
        frame.hide();
    frame.resize(frame.insets().left +
        frame.insets().right  + 320,
        frame.insets().top +
        frame.insets().bottom + 240);

    MouseClicks applet_MouseClicks = new
            MouseClicks();

    frame.add("Center", applet_MouseClicks);
    applet_MouseClicks.m_fStandAlone = true;
    applet_MouseClicks.init();
    applet_MouseClicks.start();
        frame.show();
   }

public String getAppletInfo()
   {
     return "";
   }

public void init()
   {
     resize(320, 240);
   }

public void paint(Graphics g)
   {
       g.drawString(m_Message, 10, 20);
   }

public boolean mouseDown(Event evt, int x, int y)
   {
       if ((evt.modifiers & Event.META_MASK) > 0)
         m_Message = "Clicked right mouse button";
       else
         m_Message = "Clicked left mouse button";
       // Hold Shift key down?
       if (evt.shiftDown())
         m_Message =
            " (with Shift key down) ";
       // hold Ctrl down?
       else if (evt.controlDown())
         m_Message =
            " (with Ctrl key down) ";
       m_Message =
          " @ (" + x + ", " + y + ")";
   repaint();
       return true;
   }
}
```

Tracking Mouse Moves

The AWT library offers methods that allow you to trace the mouse movement inside the drawing area and to determine when the mouse has entered or left the drawing area. The library supports the `boolean` methods `mouseEnter()`, `mouseExit()`, `mouseMove()`, and `mouseDrag()` to handle the entry, exit, movement, and dragging of the mouse, respectively. The general syntax for these methods is as follows:

```
public boolean mouseEnter(Event evt, int x, int y)
{
  statements to handle event of
  the mouse entering drawing area
  return true;
}

public boolean mouseExit(Event evt, int x, int y)
{
  statements to handle event of
  the mouse exiting drawing area
  return true;
}

public boolean mouseDrag(Event evt, int x, int y)
{
  statements to handle event of
  dragging the mouse in the drawing area
  return true;
}

public boolean mouseMove(Event evt, int x, int y)
{
  statements to handle event of
  moving the mouse in the drawing area
  return true;
}
```

The parameters for these methods are the same as those for the `mouseUp()` and `mouseDown()` methods. (See "Managing Mouse Clicks," earlier in this part.)

The methods `mouseEnter()` and `mouseExit()` represent valuable tools that allow you to determine when the mouse is inside or outside the drawing area. In addition, the parameters x and y in these methods report the coordinates for the mouse's entry and exit.

The following is a test program that displays the current mouse coordinates when the mouse is inside the drawing area. When you move the mouse outside the drawing area, the program displays a message inside the drawing area telling you that the mouse exited. When you move the mouse inside the drawing area, the program displays a message inside the drawing area telling you that the mouse entered. The program removes this message after you move the mouse inside the drawing area.

```java
import java.awt.*;

public class UseMouseMove extends Applet
{
  protected String m_TopMessage = new String();
  protected String m_BotMessage = new String();
  protected int m_nCount;

  public String getAppletInfo()
  {
    return "";
  }


  public void init()
  {
    resize(320, 240);
    m_nCount = 0;
  }

  public void paint(Graphics g)
  {
    g.drawString(m_TopMessage, 10, 20);
    g.drawString(m_BotMessage, 10, 200);
  }


  public boolean mouseMove(Event evt, int x, int y)
  {
    m_TopMessage = "Mouse at (" + x +
                   ", " + y + ")";
    if (m_nCount <= 0)
      m_BotMessage = "";
    else
      m_nCount--;
    repaint();
    return true;
  }

  public boolean mouseEnter(Event evt, int x, int
   y)
  {
    m_BotMessage = "Mouse has entered!";
    m_nCount = 50;
    repaint();
    return true;
  }

  public boolean mouseExit(Event evt, int x, int y)
  {
```

(continued)

(continued)

```
    m_BotMessage = "Mouse has exited!";
    m_TopMessage = "";
    repaint();
    return true;
}

}
```

The next figure shows a sample session with the mouse-movement test program.

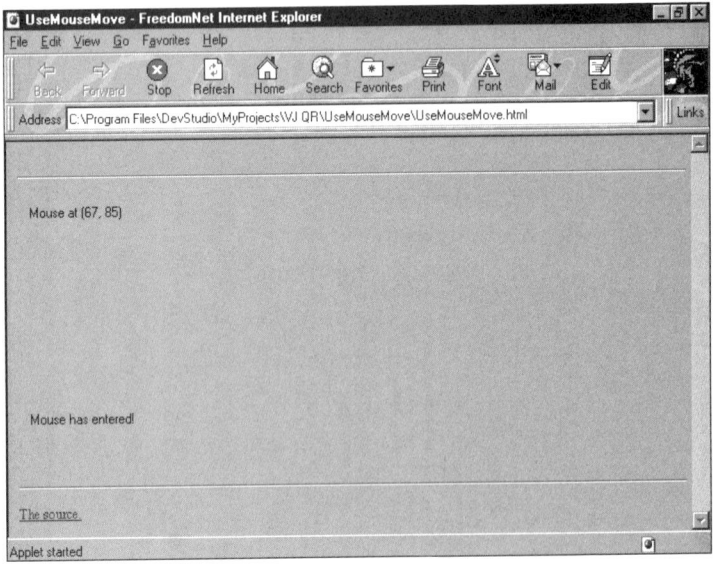

The previous source code declares the class UseMouseMove, which contains the following attributes:

+ The String-type attribute m_TopMessage stores the message that tells you where you clicked the mouse. The program displays the text of this attribute near the top of the drawing area.

+ The String-type attribute m_BotMessage stores the message that tells you when the mouse entered or exited. The program displays the text of this attribute near the bottom of the drawing area.

+ The int-type attribute m_nCount stores the number of times the runtime system invokes the method mouseMove() before the program clears the text of the attribute m_BotMessage.

The next sections describe the methods of the class UseMouseMove.

The method init ( )

The method init() performs the following tasks:

+ Resizes the drawing area

+ Initializes the attribute m_nCount

The method paint ( )

The method paint() performs the following tasks:

+ Displays the text in the attribute m_TopMessage. This task sends the message drawString() to the object g. The arguments for this message are the attribute m_TopMessage and the coordinates 10 and 20.

+ Displays the text in the attribute m_BotMessage. This task sends the message drawString() to the object g. The arguments for this message are the attribute m_BotMessage and the coordinates 10 and 200.

The method mouseMove ( )

The method mouseMove() responds to moving the mouse. This method performs the following tasks:

+ Assigns a new string in the attribute m_TopMessage. This new text reflects the current mouse coordinates.

+ Examines the value in the attribute m_nCount. When this attribute stores zero or less, the method assigns an empty string to the attribute m_TopMessage. Otherwise, the method decreases the value of the attribute m_nCount by 1.

+ Repaints the drawing area.

+ Returns true.

The method mouseEnter ( )

The method mouseEnter() responds to the event that is generated when the mouse enters the drawing area. This method performs the following tasks:

+ Assigns the string literal "Mouse has entered!" to the attribute m_BotMessage.

✦ Assigns 50 to the attribute m_nCount. This number represents the number of times that the method mouseMove() is called before it erases the message "Mouse has entered!".

✦ Repaints the drawing area.

✦ Returns true.

The method mouseExit ( )

The method mouseExit() responds to the event that is generated when the mouse exits the drawing area. This method performs the following tasks:

✦ Assigns the string literal "Mouse has exited!" to the attribute m_BotMessage.

✦ Assigns an empty string to the attribute m_TopMessage.

✦ Repaints the drawing area.

✦ Returns true.

## Part X

Basic Controls

This part presents the reference for basic visual controls that you can display on a Web page. These commonly used controls include labels, buttons, check boxes, text fields, and text areas. The text summarizes the relevant constructors and methods for each control and offers you a short test program to show you the controls at work.

In this part

✔ **Working with buttons**

✔ **Using check boxes**

✔ **Using labels**

✔ **Working with text fields and text area controls**

Buttons

The button presents a visual control that allows the user to perform tasks by clicking the button. The Java AWT library offers the class Button to support the button control. This class defines the constructor and methods that allow you to create labels with the text that you specify and the alignment of your choice. The following table shows the constructor and methods that are relevant to you as a Java programmer.

Constructor/Method	Purpose
Button(String label)	Creates a button with a specified label.
public void setLabel(String label)	Sets the control's label.
public String getLabel()	Returns the control's label.

The class Button (as with all other visual controls) inherits the parameterless methods show(), hide(), enable(), and disable() to show, hide, enable, and disable buttons, respectively.

The following code shows an example for creating buttons:

```
MyFrame(String title)
{
   ...
   // declare and create the buttons
   Button QuitBtn = new Button("Quit");
   Button OpenBtn = new Button("Open File");

   ...
   // add the controls to the frame window
   add(QuitBtn);
   add(OpenBtn);
   ...
}
```

This example declares and creates the buttons QuitBtn and OpenBtn. The example creates these controls by using the default (and only) constructor that belongs to the class Button. This code also adds these buttons to the frame window by sending the message add() to that window.

Use the method getLabel() to identify the buttons when you respond to events.

I also present a simple programming example. I created this program using the general steps discussed in Part I in the section "The Java Applet Wizard." The next example shows a Web page with two buttons, labeled Hello and Reset, and a label. This label shows the initial text Click a button. When you click the Hello button, the program displays the message You clicked the Hello button in the label. When you click the Reset button, the program displays the message Click a button.

The following is the Java source code for the button test program:

```java
import java.applet.*;
import java.awt.*;

public class UseButtons extends Applet
{
  protected Button m_HelloBtn = new
    Button("Hello");
  protected Button m_ResetBtn = new
    Button("Reset");
protected String m_Message = new
        String("Click a button");

public String getAppletInfo()
{ return ""; }

public void init()
  {
resize(320, 240);
        // add buttons
    add(m_HelloBtn);
    add(m_ResetBtn);
  }

public void paint(Graphics g)
  {
    g.drawString(m_Message, 10, 50);
  }

public boolean action(Event evt, Object arg)
  {
      if (evt.target instanceof Button) {
        String text = (String)arg;
        if (text.equals("Hello")) {
          m_Message = "You clicked the Hello
    button";
      }
        else if (text.equals("Reset")) {
          m_Message = "Click a button";
      }
        repaint();
    }
      return true;
  }
}
```

This code declares the class `UseButtons`, which declares the following attributes:

+ The `Button`-type attribute `m_HelloBtn` supports the Hello button.

+ The `Button`-type attribute `m_ResetBtn` supports the Reset button.

✦ The String-type attribute m_Message displays the program's message.

The next sections discuss the relevant class methods.

The method init ( )

The method init() adds the two buttons in the drawing area. This method sends the add() message to the applet to add these controls. The arguments for these messages are the names of the attributes, m_HelloBtn and m_ResetBtn, which support the added buttons.

The method paint ( )

The method paint() displays the text in the attribute m_Message by sending the message drawString to the graphics object g.

The method action ( )

The method action() responds to the clicking of a mouse button on one of the button controls. The method uses an if statement to examine the condition (evt.target instanceof Button) and determine whether the event was generated by a button. If this condition is true, the method uses a multiple-alternative if statement to determine which button you clicked. The following are the possible scenarios:

✦ If you clicked the Hello button, the method assigns the string You clicked the Hello button to the attribute m_Message to indicate that you clicked the Hello button.

✦ If you clicked the Reset button, the method assigns the string Click a button to the attribute m_Message to indicate that you clicked the Reset button.

Check Boxes

The class Checkbox supports both the check box and the button control. This class offers a constructor and several methods. The following table shows the constructor and methods that are relevant to you as a Java programmer.

Constructor/Method	Purpose
Checkbox(String label)	Creates a check box with a label. The default state is unchecked.

Constructor/Method	Purpose
Checkbox(String label, CheckboxGroup group, boolean state)	Creates a check box that is logically connected with the checkbox group control `group`. The parameter `state` specifies whether the radio button is selected. Creates a check box (when the argument for the parameter `group` is `null`). The parameter `state` specifies whether the check box is selected.
public void setLabel (String label)	Sets the control's label.
public String getLabel()	Returns the control's label.
public void setState (boolean state)	Sets the control's selection state.
public boolean getState()	Returns the control's selection state.

The following sample code shows an example of creating a checkbox group control and a set of buttons that are logically connected to the group control:

```
MyFrame(String title)
{
  ...
  // declare and create the group control
  CheckboxGroup MoneyTypeGrp = new CheckboxGroup();
  // declare and create the radio buttons
  Checkbox DollarRad = new Checkbox("Dollars",
    MoneyTypeGrp, true);
  Checkbox YenRad = new Checkbox("Yens",
    MoneyTypeGrp, false);
  Checkbox DinnarRad = new Checkbox("Dinnars",
                                    MoneyTypeGrp,
    false);
  ...
  // add the controls to the frame window
  add(DollarRad);
  add(YenRad);
  add(DinnarRad);
  ...
}
```

This example declares and creates the group control `MoneyTypeGrp` and declares and creates the buttons `DollarRad`, `YenRad`, and `DinnarRad`. The code logically connects these buttons to the group control `MoneyTypeGrp` by using the name of that control as the second argument for the constructor `Checkbox`. This example shows that the `DollarRad` button is selected, because the third argument for its constructor is `true` (whereas the third argument for the other control's constructors is `false`). The last three statements in the preceding example add the buttons to the frame window.

The next code sample shows an example of creating a set of check boxes:

```
MyFrame(String title)
{
    ...
    // declare and create the check boxes
    Checkbox WholeChk = new Checkbox("Whole Word",
      null, false);
    Checkbox SelectionChk = new Checkbox("Selected
      Text",
      null, false);
    Checkbox ForwardChk = new Checkbox("Forward",
      null, false);
    ...
    // add the controls to the frame window
    add(WholeChk);
    add(SelectionChk);
    add(ForwardChk);
    ...
}
```

This example declares and creates the check boxes WholeChk, SelectionChk, and ForwardChk. Notice that the example creates these controls with the arguments null and false supplied to the constructors. The last three statements in the preceding example add the check boxes to the frame window.

Use the postfix or prefix names, such as Chk and Rad, to distinguish between check boxes and button controls. These prefixes make your source code easier to read.

The next program demonstrates the use of the class CheckBox to support the button and check box controls. This program displays two buttons, labeled Uppercase and Lowercase, and a check box labeled Use alternate text, along with the initial text Hello World!. When you click the Uppercase button, the text becomes HELLO WORLD!. Then, when you click the Lowercase button, the text becomes hello world!. When you click the check box, the text becomes java is cool! (or JAVA IS COOL!) The following figure shows a sample session with the test program. If you select the Use alternate text checkbox before selecting one of the radio buttons, the text will be Java is cool!.

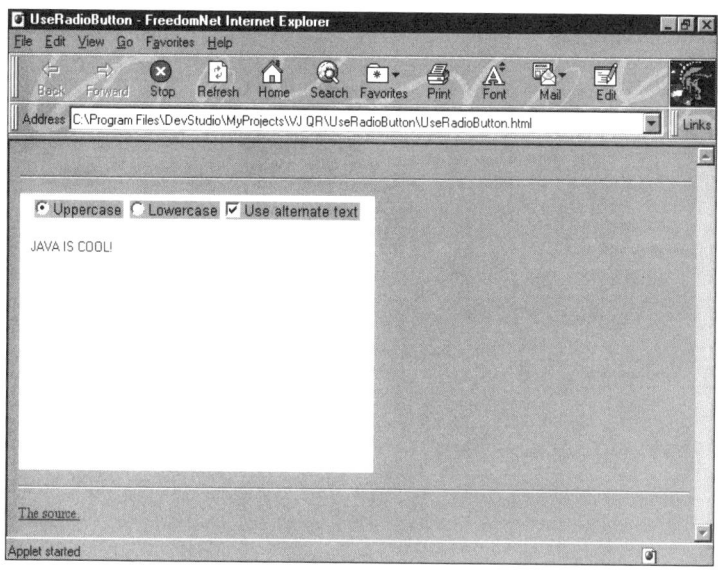

```
import java.applet.*;
import java.awt.*;

public class UseRadioButton extends Applet
{
    protected final String MSG1 = "Hello World!";
    protected final String MSG2 = "Java is cool!";
    protected CheckboxGroup m_CaseGrp;
    protected Checkbox m_UppercaseRad;
    protected Checkbox m_LowercaseRad;
    protected Checkbox m_AltTextChk;

public String getAppletInfo()
  {
    return "";
  }


public void init()
  {
resize(320, 240);

    setBackground(Color.white);
        // create, initialize, and add the controls
        m_CaseGrp = new CheckboxGroup();
        m_UppercaseRad = new Checkbox("Uppercase",
         m_CaseGrp, false);
        m_LowercaseRad = new Checkbox("Lowercase",
         m_CaseGrp, false);
        m_AltTextChk = new Checkbox("Use alternate
    text",
```

(continued)

(continued)

```
            null, false);

        // add the controls
        add(m_UppercaseRad);
        add(m_LowercaseRad);
        add(m_AltTextChk);
    }

public void paint(Graphics g)
    {
        String str;

        str = (m_AltTextChk.getState()) ?
            MSG2 : MSG1;

        if (m_UppercaseRad.getState())
            str = str.toUpperCase();
        else if (m_LowercaseRad.getState())
            str = str.toLowerCase();
        g.drawString(str, 10, 50);
    }

    public boolean action(Event evt, Object arg)
    {
        if (evt.target instanceof Checkbox)
            repaint();
        return true;
    }
}
```

This code declares the class UseRadioButton to support the buttons and check box that appear in the test program. The class declares the following attributes:

+ The final String-type attribute MSG1, which has the string literal Hello World! associated with it.

+ The final String-type attribute MSG2, which has the string literal Java is cool! associated with it.

+ The object m_CaseGrp, which has the type class CheckboxGroup.

+ The object m_UppercaseRad, which has the type class Checkbox. This attribute supports the Uppercase button.

+ The object m_LowercaseRad, which has the type class Checkbox. This attribute supports the Lowercase button.

+ The object m_AlttextChk, which has the type class Checkbox. This attribute supports the Use alternate text check box.

The next sections discuss the methods in the class UseRadioButton.

The method init ( )

The method init( ) performs the following tasks:

✦ Sets the background color of the drawing area to white.

✦ Creates the object for the attribute m_CaseGrp. This task invokes the operator new and the constructor CheckboxGroup.

✦ Creates the object for the attribute m_UppercaseRad. This task, which yields the Uppercase button, invokes the operator new and the constructor Checkbox. The invocation of the constructor specifies the control's label, the parent group control m_CaseGrp, and a false initial selection state.

✦ Creates the object for the attribute m_LowercaseRad. This task, which yields the Lowercase button, invokes the operator new and the constructor Checkbox. The invocation of the constructor specifies the control's label, the parent group control m_CaseGrp, and a false initial selection state.

✦ Creates the object for attribute m_AltTextChk. This task, which yields the Use alternate text check box, invokes the operator new and the constructor Checkbox. The invocation of the constructor specifies the control's label, the pointer null, and a false initial selection state.

✦ Adds the Uppercase button to the frame by sending the message add( ) to that frame. The argument for this message is the object m_UppercaseRad.

✦ Adds the Lowercase button to the frame by sending the message add( ) to that frame. The argument for this message is the object m_LowercaseRad.

✦ Adds the check box to the frame by sending the message add( ) to that frame. The argument for this message is the object m_AltTextChk.

The method paint ( )

The method paint( ) displays the text in a manner that conforms to the currently selected button. This method declares the local variable str and assigns the string in either attributes MSG2 or MSG1, depending on the selection state of the check box. The method sends the message getState( ) to that check box to obtain its selection state. This method uses a multiple-alternative if statement to determine which button is selected (and displays the text in three states: original, uppercase, and lowercase) by performing the following tasks:

✦ Determines whether the Uppercase button is selected. This task examines the `boolean` result of sending the message `getState()` to the Uppercase button. If that condition is true, the method sends the message `toUpperCase()` to the variable `str` and stores the resulting uppercase string back in `str`.

✦ Determines whether the Lowercase button is selected. This task examines the `boolean` result of sending the message `getState()` to the Lowercase button. If that condition is true, the method sends the message `toLowerCase()` to the variable `str` and stores the resulting uppercase string back in `str`.

✦ Displays the characters in the variable `str`.

The method action ( )

The method `action()` responds to the selection of a new button or clicking on the check box. This method uses an `if` statement to examine the condition (`evt.target instanceof Checkbox`) and determine if the event was generated by a button or a check box. If this condition is true, the method repaints the frame's drawing area by invoking the method `repaint()`. This method, in turn, invokes the method `paint()`, which determines how the greeting message appears.

Labels

The static text control (also called a *label*) allows you to place text on a Web page that typically labels a control, shows an error message, or displays a reminder. The Java AWT library offers the class `Label` to support the static text control. This class defines constructors and methods that allow you to create labels with the text that you specify and the alignment of your choice. The following table shows the constructors and relevant methods:

Constructor/Method	Purpose
Label(String label)	Creates a label with a specified text. The text for the control is left aligned.
Label(String label, int alignment)	Creates a label with a specified text and alignment.
public void setText (String label)	Sets the control's text.
public String getText()	Returns the control's text.

Constructor/Method	Purpose
public void setAlignment (int alignment)	Sets the control's alignment.
public int getAlignment()	Returns the control's alignment.

The class Label declares the constants CENTER, LEFT, and RIGHT to support centered, left, and right text alignment, respectively.

The following is an example that demonstrates how to create static text controls:

```
MyFrame(String title)
{
  ...
  // declare and create the static text controls
  Label Lbl1 = new Label("This label");
  // next control has centered text
  Label Lbl2 = new Label("Center label",
    Label.CENTER);
  Label Lbl3 = new Label("Left label", Label.LEFT);
  Label Lbl4 = new Label("Right label",
    Label.RIGHT);
  ...
  // add the controls to the frame window
  add(Lbl1);
  add(Lbl2);
  add(Lbl3);
  add(Lbl4);
  ...
}
```

This example declares and creates the static text controls Lbl1, Lbl2, Lbl3, and Lbl4. The example demonstrates the following items:

✦ The creation of the first control uses the default constructor. The text for the control is left aligned by default.

✦ The creation of the second control uses the constructor Label(String, int) and the value Label.CENTER, which specifies that the text is centered.

✦ The creation of the third control uses the constructor Label(String, int) and the value Label.LEFT, which specifies that the text is left aligned.

✦ The creation of the fourth control uses the constructor Label(String, int) and the value Label.RIGHT, which specifies that the text is right aligned.

The example also adds these controls to the frame window by sending a series of the message add() to that window. The argument for each message is one of the label controls.

 Use the methods `getText()` and/or `getAlignment()` to identify the labels when you respond to events.

The Text Field and Text Area Controls

The text field and text area controls support the user's input to Web pages. The text field (also known as the *text box, edit box,* and *edit field*) allows you to enter a single row or line of text. By contrast, the text area supports multiple rows or lines of text. The Java AWT library offers the classes `TextComponent`, `TextField`, and `TextArea` to support the text field and text area controls. The class `TextComponent` is the parent of the classes `TextField` and `TextArea`.

The following table shows the methods for the class `TextComponent`.

Method	Purpose
public String getSelectedText()	Returns the selected text.
public int getSelectionEnd()	Returns the character index for the end of the selection.
public int getSelectionStart()	Returns the character index for the start of the selection.
public String getText()	Returns the control's text.
public boolean isEditable()	Yields a logical flag to indicate whether you can edit the text in a text field or text area.
public void select(int selStart, int selEnd)	Selects text that is specified by the character indices `selStart` and `selEnd`.
public void selectAll()	Selects all of the text.
public void setEditable(boolean flag)	Turns on or off the ability to edit the text in a text field or text area.
public void setText(String text)	Sets the text to the value of the parameter `text`.

The following table shows the constructors and methods for the class `TextField`.

Constructor/Method	Purpose
public TextField()	The default constructor that creates a new text field with no text.
public TextField(int cols)	Creates a text field with space for `cols` characters (also called *the number of columns*) but no text.

Constructor/Method	Purpose
public TextField(String text)	Creates a text field with the text specified by the parameter `text`.
public TextField(String text, int cols)	Creates a text field with the text specified by the parameter `text` and with space for `cols` characters (also called *the number of columns*).
public int getColumns( )	Yields the number of columns.

The following table shows the constructors and methods for the class `TextArea`:

public TextArea()	The default constructor that creates a new text area with no text.
public TextArea(int rows, int cols)	Creates a text field with space for `cols` number of columns and `rows` number of rows, but no text.
public TextArea(String text)	Creates a text area with the text specified by the parameter `text`.
public TextArea(String text, int rows, int cols)	Creates a text area with the text specified by the parameter `text`, and with `cols` number of columns and `rows` number of rows.
public int getColumns( )	Yields the number of columns.
public int getRows( )	Yields the number of rows.
public void appendText (String appText)	Appends the text specified by the parameter `appText` to the current contents of the text area.
public void insertText (String insText, int pos)	Inserts the text that is specified by the parameter `insText` at the character index that is specified by the parameter `pos`.
public void replaceText(String newText, int startPos, int endPos)	Replaces the characters `startPos` to `endPos` with the value of the parameter `newText`.

The following code shows an example of creating text field and text area controls:

```
MyFrame(String title)
{
   ...
   // declare and create the text fields
   TextField findTxt = new TextField("this");
   TextField replTxt = new TextField("that", 10);
   // declare and create the text area
   TextArea TextEdt = new TextArea(15, 10);
   ...
   // add the controls to the frame window
   add(findTxt);
   add(replTxt);
```

(continued)

(continued)
```
   add(TextEdt);
   ...
}
```

This example declares and creates the text field controls findTxt and replTxt. The example creates the object findTxt by using the constructor TextField(String) to assign the initial string "this" to the control. Then the example creates the object replTxt by using the constructor TextField(String, int) to assign the initial string "that" to the control and to reserve ten columns in the control. The code creates the text area control TextEdt by using the constructor TextArea(String, int, int). This control shows 15 rows and 10 columns, but has no text initially.

The method replaceText() allows you to delete text by passing an empty string to the parameter newText. The arguments for parameters startPos and endPos specify the range of characters to delete.

The following program uses the text field and text area controls. This program displays buttons labeled Find and Replace, two text fields, and a text area. The program uses static text controls to label the text fields as Find: and Replace: and to label the text area control as Text:. The program supports the following features:

♦ When you click the Find button, the program uses the text in the Find text field to search for a match in the text area. If the program finds a match, it selects that match. The search is case sensitive.

♦ When you click the Replace button, the program uses the text in the Find text field to search for a match in the text area. If the program finds a match, it replaces that text with the contents of the Replace text field. The search and replacement are case sensitive.

```
import java.applet.*;
import java.awt.*;

public class UseText extends Applet
{
  protected Label m_FindLbl = new Label("Find:");
  protected Label m_ReplaceLbl = new
    Label("Replace:");
  protected Label m_TextLbl = new Label("Text:");
  protected TextField m_FindTxt = new
    TextField(40);
  protected TextField m_ReplaceTxt = new
    TextField(35);
```

```java
protected TextArea m_TextEdt = new TextArea(10,
  25);
protected Button m_ReplaceBtn = new
  Button("Replace");
protected Button m_FindBtn = new Button("Find");
protected int m_nIndex = -1;

public String getAppletInfo()
{
  return "";
}

public void init()
{
  resize(320, 240);

  // add controls
  add(m_FindLbl);
  add(m_FindTxt);
  add(m_ReplaceLbl);
  add(m_ReplaceTxt);
  add(m_TextLbl);
  add(m_TextEdt);
  add(m_FindBtn);
  add(m_ReplaceBtn);

  // insert text
  m_FindTxt.setText("C++");
  m_ReplaceTxt.setText("Java");
  m_TextEdt.setText("language for ");
  m_TextEdt.insertText("C++ is the best \n", 0);
  m_TextEdt.appendText("the Web!");
}

public int findText(TextField FindTxt,
                    TextArea TextEdt,
                    int index)
{
  String findStr;
  String textStr;
  findStr = FindTxt.getText();
  textStr = TextEdt.getText();

  // any text to find?
  if (findStr.length() > 0 &&
    textStr.length() > 0) {
    // get the index of the next occurrence
    index = textStr.indexOf(findStr, index + 1);
    if (index > -1)
      TextEdt.select(index,
      index + findStr.length());
    else
      TextEdt.select(-1,0);
    TextEdt.requestFocus();
  }
  return index;
```

(continued)

(continued)

```
   }

public void replaceText(TextField FindTxt,
                        TextField ReplTxt,
                        TextArea TextEdt)
{
  String findStr;
  String replStr;
  String textStr;
  int nIndex ;

  findStr = FindTxt.getText();
  replStr = ReplTxt.getText();
  textStr = TextEdt.getText();

  // any text to replace?
  if (findStr.length() > 0 &&
    textStr.length() > 0) {
    // get the index of the first occurrence
    nIndex = textStr.indexOf(findStr);
    while (nIndex > -1) {
      TextEdt.replaceText(replStr, nIndex,
        nIndex + findStr.length());
      // update string in textStr
      textStr = TextEdt.getText();
      // get the index of the next occurrence
      nIndex = textStr.indexOf(findStr);
    }
  }
}

public boolean action(Event evt, Object arg)
{
  if (evt.target instanceof Button) {
    String text = (String)arg;
    if (text.equals("Find"))
      m_nIndex = findText(m_FindTxt,
      m_TextEdt,
      m_nIndex);
    else if (text.equals("Replace"))
      replaceText(m_FindTxt,
      m_ReplaceTxt,
      m_TextEdt);
    repaint();
  }
  return true;
  }
}
```

The next figure shows a sample session of the text test program.

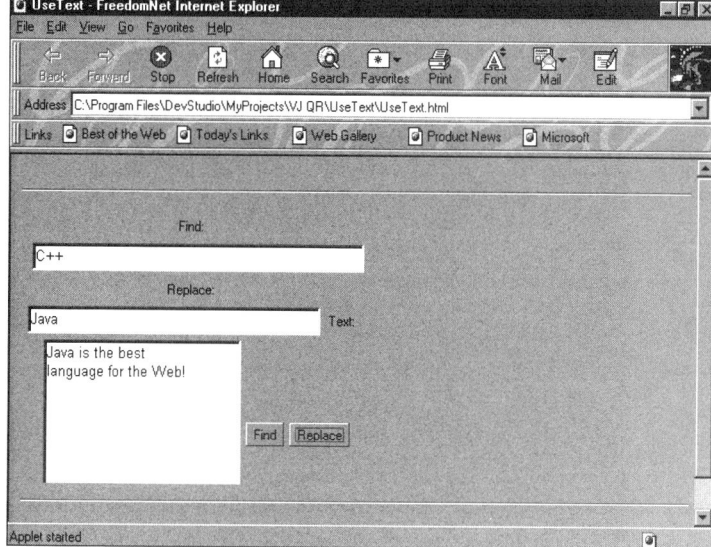

The previous source code shows the declarations and statements in the class `UseText` to support the controls that appear in this figure. The class declares the following attributes:

+ The `Label`-type attributes `m_FindLbl`, `m_ReplaceLbl`, and `m_TextLbl` support the `Find:`, `Replace:`, and `Text:` labels, respectively.

+ The `TextField`-type attributes `m_FindTxt` and `m_ReplaceTxt` support the text boxes labeled `Find:` and `Replace:`, respectively. The program creates the first text field by specifying 40 columns. Then the program specifies 35 columns for the second text field.

+ The `TextArea`-type attribute `m_TextEdt` supports the text area control. The program specifies that this control has 10 rows and 25 columns.

+ The `Button`-type attributes `m_ReplaceBtn` and `m_FindBtn` support the Replace and Find buttons, respectively.

+ The `int`-type attribute `m_nIndex` stores the character index by using the text search.

The next sections discuss the methods in the class `UseText`.

The method init ( )

The method init() performs the following tasks:

♦ Adds the labels, buttons, text fields, and text to the drawing area by sending the message add() (for each control) to that area.

♦ Sets the text of the Find: text field to fox. This task sends the message setText() to the object m_FindTxt. The argument for this message is the string literal "C++".

♦ Sets the text of the Replace: text field to cat. This task sends the message setText() to the object m_ReplaceTxt. The argument for this message is the string literal "Javacat".

♦ Sets the text of the Text: text area to language for. This task sends the message setText() to the object m_textEdt. The argument for this message is the string literal "language for ".

♦ Inserts the string literal "C++ is the best \n" at the beginning of the text in the text area. This task sends the message insertText() to the object m_textEdt. The arguments for this message are the inserted string literal and the character index 0.

♦ Appends the string literal "the Web!" to the end of the text in the text area. This task sends the message appendText() to the object m_textEdt. The argument for this message is the appended string literal.

The method action ( )

The method action() responds to the clicking of a button. This method uses an if statement to examine the condition (evt.target instanceof Button) and determine if the event was generated by a button. If this condition is true, the method uses a multiple-alternative if statement to determine which button you clicked. The following are the possible scenarios:

♦ If you click the Find button, the method searches for text by invoking the method findText().

♦ If you click the Replace button, the method replaces text by invoking the method replaceText().

The method findText ( )

The method findText() responds to clicking the Find button by searching for the text in the text area control. This method performs the following tasks:

✦ Copies the text of the Find: text field to the local string variable findStr. This task sends the message getText() to the object m_FindTxt.

✦ Copies the text of the Text: text field to the local string variable textStr. This task sends the message getText() to the object m_TextEdt.

✦ Performs the subsequent tasks if both of the variables findStr and textStr do not contain empty strings. These tasks use an if statement that examines the condition of sending the message length() to each of the two variables to obtain the number of characters in these variables.

✦ Obtains the character index of the next occurrence of the search string (stored in the variable findStr) in the text area (whose copy is stored in the variable textStr). This task sends the message indexOf() to the local variable textStr. The arguments for this message are the variable findStr and the expression m_nIndex + 1. This expression tells the message where to start searching.

✦ Determines whether the search (performed in the preceding task) is successful. The method uses an if statement to determine if the attribute m_nIndex stores a character index that is greater than –1 (the message indexOf() returns –1 if it finds no match). When this condition is true, the method selects the text in the range of m_nIndex and m_nIndex + findStr.length(). The method sends the message select() to the object m_TextEdt to select the targeted text. The arguments for this message are the attribute m_nIndex and the expression m_nIndex + findStr.length(). If the search fails, the method deselects text by sending the message select() to the object m_TextEdt with the arguments –1 and 0.

✦ Sets the focus to the text area (to display any selected text). This task sends the message requestFocus() to the object m_TextEdt.

The method replaceText ( )

The method replaceText() responds to clicking the Replace button and replaces text in the text area by using the search and replacement strings that appear in the Find: and Replace: text fields, respectively. The method performs the following tasks:

✦ Copies the text of the Find: text field to the local string variable findStr. This task sends the message getText() to the object m_FindTxt.

✦ Copies the text of the Replace: text field to the local string variable replStr. This task sends the message getText() to the object m_ReplaceTxt.

✦ Copies the text of the Text: text field to the local string variable textStr. This task sends the message getText() to the object m_TextEdt.

✦ Performs the subsequent tasks if both of the variables findStr and textStr do not contain empty strings. These tasks use an if statement that examines the condition of sending the message length() to each of the two variables to obtain the number of characters in these variables.

✦ Obtains the character index of the first occurrence of the search string (stored in the variable findStr) in the text area (whose copy is stored in the variable textStr). This task sends the message indexOf() to the local variable textStr. The argument for this message is the variable findStr. This task stores the character index in the local int-type variable nIndex.

✦ Uses a while loop to replace all matching text. This loop iterates as long as there is text to replace. The logical expression nIndex > -1 supports this condition. The loop performs the subsequent tasks.

✦ Replaces the targeted text. This task sends the message replaceText() to the object m_TextEdt. The arguments for this message are the replacement string (stored in the variable replStr) and the range of indices defined by the variable nIndex and the expression nIndex + findStr.length().

✦ Obtains an updated copy of the Text: text field and stores it in the local string variable textStr. This task sends the message getText() to the object m_TextEdt.

✦ Obtains the character index of the next occurrence of the search string (stored in the variable findStr) in the text area (whose copy is stored in the variable textStr). This task sends the message indexOf() to the local variable textStr. The argument for this message is the variable findStr. This task stores the character index in the local int-type variable nIndex.

## Part XI

Scrollable Controls

This part looks at scrollable controls, which allow you to select from a wide range of values or from a set of items. Scrollable controls include the scrollbar and the list box. The scrollbar controls allows you to quickly select a value from a wide range of integers. The list box control allows you to pick the name of an item from a set of names, without having to remember these names. The list box allows you to choose from a predefined set of names. This part also shows you how to work with list boxes that support single selections and multiple selections.

In this part

✔ Working with scrollbars

✔ Using single-selection list boxes

✔ Working with multiple-selection list boxes

List Boxes

List boxes are popular controls in user-friendly applications because they save you from having to remember the exact names (and spellings) of a variety of items (states, colors, countries, and so on). The Java AWT offers the class List to support lists of strings. This class supports single-selection and multiple-selection lists. In a single-selection list, you can select only one item. By contrast, in a multiple-selection list you can select any number of items. The flexibility of multiple-selection lists includes the ability to add more items to the selection and to deselect current items.

The following two tables present the constructors and methods of the class List. The first table shows you the constructor and methods that work with both single-selection and multiple-selection lists. The second table focuses on the methods that manage single-selection lists.

Constructor/Method	Purpose
public List(int numVisibleRows, boolean multipleSelections)	Creates a list control that displays numVisible visible rows. The multipleSelection parameter allows you to select between creating a single-selection or a multiple-selection list.
public void addItem(String item)	Adds an item to the end of the scrolling list.
public void addItem (String item, int index)	Adds an item to the specified index of the scrolling list. The index of the first item is 0. Supplying an argument of −1 for the parameter index places the added item at the end of the list.
public void clear()	Removes all of the items from the scrolling list.
public int countItems()	Returns the number of items in the scrolling list.
public void delItem(int index)	Deletes an item from the list by specifying the item's index.
public void delItem (int first, int last)	Deletes a range of items from the list by specifying the item's first and last indices.
public String getItem(int index)	Returns an item from the list by specifying the index of that item.
public boolean isSelected(int index)	Determines whether an item (specified by index) is selected.

Constructor/Method	Purpose
public void replaceItem (String newItem, int index)	Replaces the item at the specified index with the new item that is designated by the parameter newItem.
public void select (int index)	Selects an item that is specified by index.
public void setMultipleSelections (boolean multipleSelections)	Turns on or off multiple-selection mode for a scrolling list.
public boolean allowMultipleSelections()	Returns true if the list allows multiple selections. Otherwise, it yields false.

The following code shows a general example for creating a scrolling list:

```
MyFrame(String title)
{
    ...
    // declare and create the scrolling list
    List NamesLst = new List(10, false);
    // add items
    NamesLst.addItem("Bonjour!");
    ...
    // add control to frame
    add(NamesLst);
    ...
    // select the first item
    NamesLst.select(0);
}
```

This example declares and creates the single-selection scrolling list NamesLst, which displays up to ten rows. The code also adds items to the list by sending the message addItems() to the object NamesLst. Next, the example adds the scrolling list to the frame window and then selects the first list item. This task involves sending the message select() to the object NamesLst. The argument for this message is 0, the index of the first item.

The two versions of method addItems do not store items in a sorted order. You're responsible for inserting them in order if you want to display them in order. In addition, these methods do not prohibit the list from having duplicate items. Again, you're responsible for ensuring that your applet does not insert duplicate items.

Multiple-Selection Lists

The following table shows you the few methods that are specific to multiple-selection lists.

Method	Purpose
public synchronized int[ ] getSelectedIndexes()	Returns the array of indices for the selected items.
public synchronized Stringp[ ] getSelectedItems()	Returns the array of selected items.

The following is a programming example that uses a multiple-selection list. The program displays the following controls:

✦ The multiple-selection list box labeled Names List, which displays a set of names

✦ The single-selection list box labeled Selected Names, which displays the selections in the Names List control

✦ The Get Names button, which allows you to copy the selections in the Names List control to the Selected Names control

✦ The single-selection list labeled Selected Indices, which displays the indices of the selections in the Names List control

✦ The Get Indices button, which allows you to copy the indices of the selections in the Names List control to the Selected Indices control

✦ The Clear Selections button, which permits you to clear the selections in the Names List control

When you create this example using the Java Applet Wizard, you also need to set the size of the frame in the USEMULTILIST.HTML and USEMULTILIST.JAVA files to have a width and length of 600 and 2,840 pixels, respectively. The following figure shows a sample session using the multiple-selection list program.

```
import java.applet.*;
import java.awt.*;

public class UseMultiList extends Applet
{
  protected List m_NamesLst = new List(10, true);
  protected List m_SelNameLst = new List(4, false);
  protected List m_SelIndexLst = new List(4,
    false);
  protected Label m_NamesLbl = new Label("Names
    List");
  protected Label m_SelNameLbl =
    new Label("Selected Names");
  protected Label m_SelIndexLbl =
    new Label("Selected Indices");
  protected Button m_GetNamesBtn =
    new Button("Get Names");
  protected Button m_GetIndicesBtn =
    new Button("Get Indices");
  protected Button m_ClearSelBtn =
```

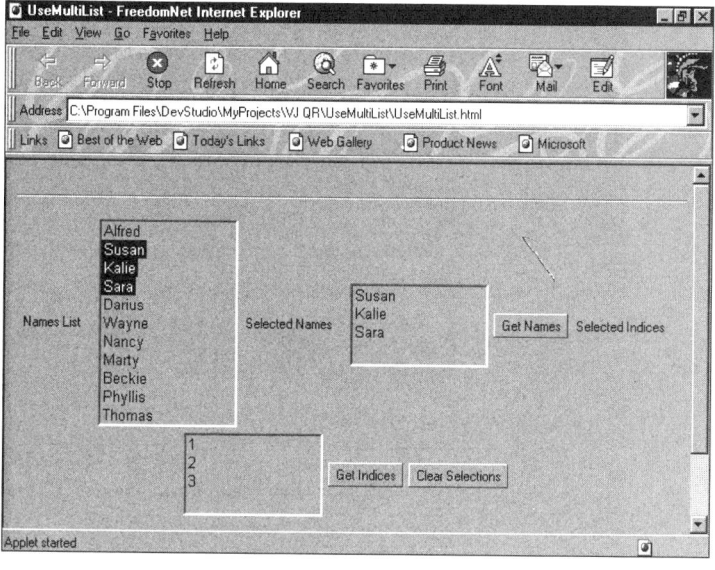

```
    new Button("Clear Selections");

public String getAppletInfo()
  {
    return "";
  }


public void init()
  {
      resize(600, 280);

      m_NamesLst.addItem("Alfred");
      m_NamesLst.addItem("Susan");
      m_NamesLst.addItem("Kalie");
      m_NamesLst.addItem("Sara");
      m_NamesLst.addItem("Darius");
      m_NamesLst.addItem("Wayne");
      m_NamesLst.addItem("Nancy");
      m_NamesLst.addItem("Marty");
      m_NamesLst.addItem("Beckie");
      m_NamesLst.addItem("Phyllis");
      m_NamesLst.addItem("Thomas");
      m_NamesLst.addItem("Karen");
      m_NamesLst.addItem("Marcia");

      add(m_NamesLbl);
      add(m_NamesLst);
      add(m_SelNameLbl);
      add(m_SelNameLst);
      add(m_GetNamesBtn);
```

(continued)

(continued)

```
      add(m_SelIndexLbl);
      add(m_SelIndexLst);
      add(m_GetIndicesBtn);
      add(m_ClearSelBtn);
   }

   public boolean action(Event evt, Object arg) {
      int nIdx;
      String text = (String)arg;

      if (evt.target instanceof Button) {

         if (text.equals("Clear Selections")) {
            // get array of selected items
            int nIndex[] =
      m_NamesLst.getSelectedIndexes();
            // deselect the selected items
            for (int i = 0; i < nIndex.length; i++)
               m_NamesLst.deselect(nIndex[i]);
         }
         else if (text.equals("Get Names")) {
            // clear Selected Names box
            m_SelNameLst.clear();
            int nIndex[] =
      m_NamesLst.getSelectedIndexes();
            for (int i = 0; i < nIndex.length; i++)
               m_SelNameLst.addItem(
                  m_NamesLst.getItem(nIndex[i]));
         }
         else if (text.equals("Get Indices")) {
            // clear Selected Indices box
            m_SelIndexLst.clear();
            // get array of selected indices
            int nIndex[] =
      m_NamesLst.getSelectedIndexes();
            for (int i = 0; i < nIndex.length; i++)
               m_SelIndexLst.addItem("" + nIndex[i]);
         }
      }
      return true;
   }

}
```

This code contains the declarations and statements to the class UseMultiList that support the list and other controls that appear in the previous figure. The class declares the following attributes:

+ The multiple-selection list m_NamesLst, which displays up to ten items. This control appears next to the label Names List.

+ The single-selection list m_SelNameLst, which displays up to four items. This control appears next to the label Selected Names.

✦ The single-selection list m_SelIndexLst, which displays up to four items. This control appears next to the label Selected Indices.

✦ The label object m_NamesLbl, which has the text "Names List".

✦ The label object m_SelNameLbl, which has the text "Selected Names".

✦ The label object m_SelIndexLbl, which has the text "Selected Index".

✦ The button object m_GetNamesBtn, which has the label Get Names.

✦ The button object m_GetIndicesBtn, which has the label Get Indices.

✦ The button object m_ClearSelBtn, which has the label Clear Selections.

I also created the method action() and added statements to this method and other methods that are created by the Applet Wizard.

The method init ( )

The method init() performs the following tasks:

✦ Adds a set of names to the scrolling list. This task sends the message addItem() to object m_NamesLst to add a name. The argument for the message is the added name.

✦ Adds the lists, labels, and buttons to the drawing area.

The method action ( )

The method action() responds to any event that is generated by clicking a button. The method uses an if statement to examine the condition (evt.target instanceof Button) and determine if the event was generated by a button. If this condition is true, the method determines which button generated the event.

The Clear Selections button

The Clear Selections button causes the program to clear the selections in the Names List control. The method performs the following tasks:

✦ Stores the selections' indices in the local array nIndex. This task obtains these indices by sending the message getSelectedIndexes() to the Names List control.

◆ Deselects each selection in the Names List control. This task uses a `for` loop to access each element in the array `nIndex` and use it to deselect a list selection. The task sends the message `deselect()` to the Names List control. The argument for this message is `nIndex[i]`.

The Get Names button

The Get Names button causes the program to copy the selections from the Names List to the Selected Names control. The method performs the following tasks:

◆ Removes all items from the Selected Names control by sending the message `clear()` to that control.

◆ Stores the indices of the selections (in the Names List control) in the local array `nIndex`. This task obtains these indices by sending the message `getSelectedIndexes()` to the Names List control.

◆ Inserts the selections into the Selected Names control. This task uses a `for` loop to obtain each selection (in the Names List control) and insert it into the Selected Names control. The task obtains each selection by sending the message `getItem()` to the `Names List` control. The argument for this message is the element `nIndex[i]`. This task also inserts the selected element by sending the message `addItem()` to the Selected Names control.

The Get Indices button

The Get Indices button causes the program to copy the indices of the selections in the Names List to the Selected Indices control. The method performs the following tasks:

◆ Removes all items from the Selected Indices control by sending the message `clear()` to that control.

◆ Stores the indices of the selections (in the Names List control) in the local array `nIndex`. This task obtains these indices by sending the message `getSelectedIndexes()` to the Names List control.

◆ Inserts the indices of the selections into the Selected Indices control. This task uses a `for` loop to insert each selection index (of the Names List control) into the Selected Indices control. The task inserts the index of the selected element by sending the message `addItem()` to the Selected Indices control. The argument for this message is the expression `" " + nIndex[i]`.

Scrollbars

The scrollbar control allows you to quickly select from a relatively wide range of integers. The scrollbar contains the page gadget as well as the line-up and line-down gadgets. The control supports the following operations:

✦ Clicking the line-up gadget decreases the value of the scrollbar by a line (in most cases, 1).

✦ Clicking the line-down gadget increases the value of the scrollbar by a line.

✦ Clicking directly below the page gadget (and inside the scrollbar control) increases the value of the scrollbar by a page. (This value depends on the range and on how fast you want to move the page gadget per click.)

✦ Clicking directly above the page gadget (and inside the scrollbar control) decreases the value of the scrollbar by a page.

✦ Dragging the page gadget allows you to quickly move toward a scrollbar value that you want to select.

The Java AWT library offers the class Scrollbar to support the scrollbar control. This class offers a constructor and a number of methods. The following table shows the constructor (just one of the three class constructors) and the relevant methods.

Constructor/Method	Purpose
public Scrollbar(int orientation, int value, int visible, int minimum, int maximum)	Creates a scrollbar with either a vertical orientation (using the value ScrollBar.VERTICAL) or a horizontal orientation (using the value ScrollBar.HORIZONTAL) with the initial value and range of values (defined by the parameters minimum and maximum).
public int getValue()	Obtains the current value of the scrollbar, which is determined by the position of the page gadget.
public void setValue(int)	Sets the current value of the scrollbar, which also moves the position of the page gadget.
public void setLineIncrement (int lineIncr)	Sets the line increment (the value that is added to or subtracted from the value of the scrollbar when you click the line-down or line-up gadget).
public int getLineIncrement()	Returns the line increment value.

(continued)

Constructor/Method	Purpose
public void setPageIncrement (int pageIncr)	Sets the page increment (the value that is added to or subtracted from the value of the scrollbar when you click the page-down or page-up gadget).
public int getPageIncrement()	Returns the page increment value.
public int getMinimum()	Returns the minimum value of the scrollbar.
public int getMaximum()	Returns the maximum value of the scrollbar.
public int getOrientation()	Yields the orientation of the scrollbar (which is either Scrollbar.VERTICAL or Scrollbar.HORIZONTAL).

The following code shows a general example of creating a scrollbar control:

```
MyFrame(String title)
{
    ...
    // declare and create the scrollbar control
    Scrollbar sbr = new Scrollbar(Scrollbar.VERTICAL,
                                  0, 10, 0, 80);
    // set line and page increments
    sbr.setLineIncrement(1);
    sbr.setPageIncrement((sbr.getMaximum() -
                          sbr.getMinimum()/ 10);

    ...
    // add control to frame
    add(sbr);
    ...
}
```

This example declares and creates the vertical scrollbar control sbr with the range of values 0 to 80, the initial value 0, and the visible value of 10. The code also sets the line increment to be 1 (as expected) and the page increment to be one-tenth the range of the scrollbar values. This example sets the line and page increments by sending the messages setLineIncrement() and setPageIncrement() to the object sbr, respectively. The argument for the message setLineIncrement() is 1. The argument for the message setPageIncrement() is the expression (sbr.getMaximum() - sbr.getMinimum()/ 10). This expression sends the messages getMaximum() and getMinimum() to the object sbr to obtain the minimum and maximum scrollbar values, respectively.

The following is a test program that displays a vertical and a horizontal scrollbar. Each scrollbar control has a label that is associated with it, and that label shows the current scrollbar value. When you use the mouse to change the value of a scrollbar (for example, by clicking the up-line increment gadget), the scrollbar changes in value and the program reflects the new value in the label that is associated with that scrollbar.

```java
import java.applet.*;
import java.awt.*;

public class UseScrollbar extends Applet
{
  protected Scrollbar m_VertScr;
  protected Scrollbar m_HorzScr;
  protected Label m_VertLbl;
  protected Label m_HorzLbl;

    public String getAppletInfo()
    {
            return "";
    }


    public void init()
    {
      resize(320, 240);

      m_VertScr = new Scrollbar(Scrollbar.VERTICAL, 0,
                              10, 0, 200);
      m_HorzScr = new
    Scrollbar(Scrollbar.HORIZONTAL, 0,
                              10, 0, 200);
      m_VertLbl = new Label("0000");
      m_HorzLbl = new Label("0000");

      // set line and page increments
      m_VertScr.setLineIncrement(1);
      m_HorzScr.setLineIncrement(1);
      m_VertScr.setPageIncrement(
        (m_VertScr.getMaximum() -
        m_VertScr.getMinimum()) / 10);
      m_HorzScr.setPageIncrement(
        (m_HorzScr.getMaximum() -
        m_HorzScr.getMinimum()) / 10);

      // add controls
      add(m_HorzScr);
      add(m_HorzLbl);
      add(m_VertScr);
      add(m_VertLbl);

      // set scrollbar to median values
      m_HorzScr.setValue((m_HorzScr.getMaximum() +
        m_HorzScr.getMinimum()) / 2);
      m_VertScr.setValue((m_VertScr.getMaximum() +
        m_VertScr.getMinimum()) / 2);
```

(continued)

(continued)

```
        // update labels
        m_VertLbl.setText("" + m_VertScr.getValue());
        m_HorzLbl.setText("" + m_HorzScr.getValue());
      }

  public boolean handleEvent(Event evt)
  {
    if (evt.target instanceof Scrollbar) {
      Scrollbar sb = (Scrollbar)evt.target;
      if (sb.getOrientation() ==
  Scrollbar.VERTICAL)
        m_VertLbl.setText("" + sb.getValue());
      else
        m_HorzLbl.setText("" + sb.getValue());
      repaint();
    }
    return true;
  }
}
```

The next figure displays a sample session of the scrollbar test
program.

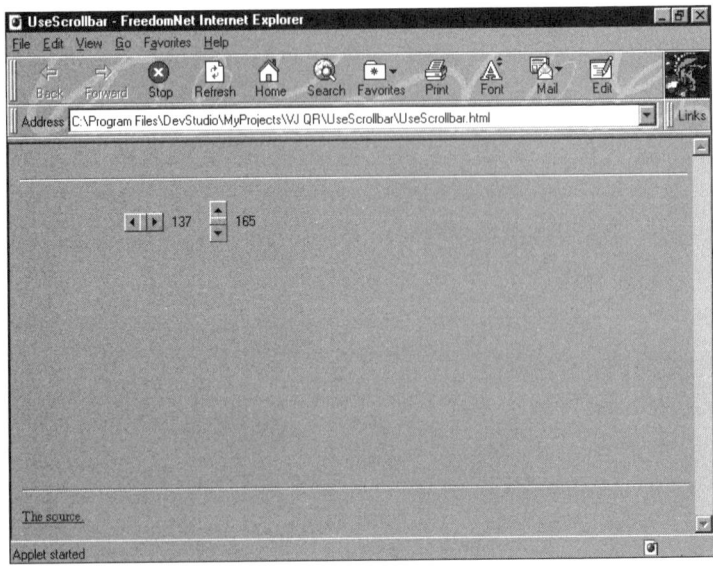

The previous source code contains the declarations and statements to the class UseScrollbar that support the scrollbars that
appear in the previous figure. The class has the following attributes:

✦ The Scrollbar-type attribute m_VertScr, which supports the vertical scrollbar

✦ The Scrollbar-type attribute m_HorzScr, which supports the horizontal scrollbar

✦ The Label-type attribute m_VertLbl, which supports the label that is associated with the vertical scrollbar

✦ The Label-type attribute m_HorzLbl, which supports the label that is associated with the horizontal scrollbar

The next sections discuss the methods in the class UseScrollbar.

The method init ( )

The method init() performs the following tasks:

✦ Creates the horizontal scrollbar object for the attribute m_HorzScr. This task invokes the operator new and the constructor Scrollbar. The argument list for this constructor is ScrollBar.HORIZONTAL, 0 (the initial scrollbar value), 10 (the visible value), and the range 0 to 200.

✦ Creates the vertical scrollbar object for the attribute m_VertScr. This task invokes the operator new and the constructor Scrollbar. The argument list for this constructor is ScrollBar.VERTICAL, 0 (the initial scrollbar value), 10 (the visible value), and the range 0 to 200.

✦ Creates the label for the attribute m_VertLbl.

✦ Creates the label for the attribute m_HorzLbl.

✦ Sets the line increment for the two scrollbar controls. This task sends the message setLineIncrement() to each scrollbar. The argument for each message is 1.

✦ Sets the page increment for the two scrollbar controls. This task sends the message setPageIncrement() to each scrollbar. The argument for each message involves sending the messages getMaximum() and getMinimum() to each scrollbar. The page increment for each scrollbar is one-tenth the range of the scrollbar values.

✦ Adds the scrollbar and label controls to the drawing area.

✦ Sets the value of each scrollbar to its median value. This task sends the message setValue() to each scrollbar. The argument for each message involves sending the messages getMaximum() and getMinimum() to each scrollbar.

✦ Updates the text of the labels that are associated with the scrollbars to reflect the new value of the scrollbar. This task sends the message setText() to each label. The argument for each message involves sending the message getValue() to a scrollbar control.

The method handleEvent ( )

The method handleEvent() responds to the event that is generated by changing the value of the scrollbars. This method uses an if statement to examine the condition (evt.target instanceof Scrollbar) and determine whether the event was generated by a scrollbar. If this condition is true, the method determines which of the two scrollbars generated the event.

The method handleEvent() uses a nested if statement to compare the constant ScrollBar.VERTICAL with the result of sending the message getOrientation() with the active scrollbar. If the active scrollbar is the vertical one, the method updates the text of label m_VertLbl with the value of the scrollbar. Otherwise, the method updates the text of label m_HorzLbl with the value of the scrollbar. In either case, the method handleEvent() obtains the scrollbar value by sending the message getValue() to that control. After updating either label, the method repaints the drawing area to show the update.

TIP

The preceding program uses a simple trick to easily convert the result of the the message getValue() into text when used with the message setText(). The trick appends the result of that message to an empty string, forcing the compiler to convert the integer into a string that looks like an integer.

Single-Selection Lists

The previous table showed you the many methods that are common to both single-selection and multiple-selection lists. The following table shows you the few methods that are specific to single-selection lists.

Method	Purpose
public int getSelectedIndex()	Returns the index of the selected item.
public String getSelectedItem()	Returns the selected item.

The next programming example uses a single list of names. The program displays the following controls:

✦ The scrolling list, which displays a list of names.

◆ The edit box labeled String. You use this control to add and
overwrite items in the list. The program also uses this control
to display the selected item.

◆ The edit box labeled Index. You use this control to select an
item by typing its index in this control. The program also uses
this control to display the index of the selected item.

◆ The Add String button. This button allows you to add the
contents of the String edit box to the list.

◆ The Delete String button. This button permits you to delete
the selected list item.

◆ The Get Selected String button. This button allows you to
copy the selected item to the String edit box.

◆ The Get Selected Index button. This button displays the index
of the selected item in the Index edit box.

The following figure shows a sample session with the single-list
test program.

```
import java.applet.*
import java.awt.*;

public class UseSingleList extends Applet
{
  protected Label m_ListBoxLbl = new Label("List
    Box");
  protected Label m_StringLbl = new
    Label("String");
  protected Label m_IndexLbl = new Label("Index");
  protected List m_NamesLst = new List(5, false);
  protected TextField m_StringTxt = new
    TextField(23);
  protected TextField m_IndexTxt = new
    TextField(23);
  protected Button m_AddStrBtn = new Button(
                            "Add String");
  protected Button m_DelStrBtn = new Button(
                            "Delete String");
  protected Button m_GetSelStrBtn = new Button(
                            "Get Selected
    String");
  protected Button m_GetSelIndexBtn = new Button(
                            "Get Selected
    Index");

public String getAppletInfo()
  {
    return "";
  }
```

(continued)

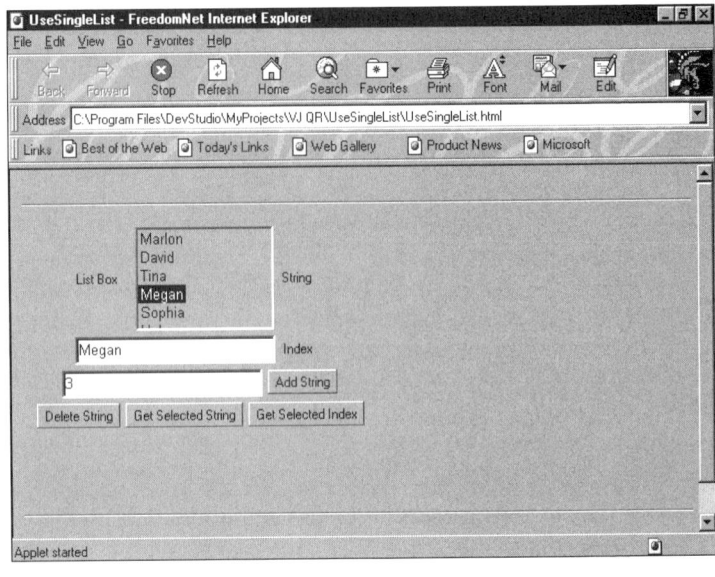

(continued)

```
public void init()
    {
        resize(320, 240);
        // add names in list box
        m_NamesLst.addItem("Marlon");
        m_NamesLst.addItem("David");
        m_NamesLst.addItem("Tina");
        m_NamesLst.addItem("Megan");
        m_NamesLst.addItem("Sophia");
        m_NamesLst.addItem("Helen");
        m_NamesLst.addItem("Julian");
        m_NamesLst.addItem("Anne");

        // add controls
        add(m_ListBoxLbl);
        add(m_NamesLst);
        add(m_StringLbl);
        add(m_StringTxt);
        add(m_IndexLbl);
        add(m_IndexTxt);
        add(m_AddStrBtn);
        add(m_DelStrBtn);
        add(m_GetSelStrBtn);
        add(m_GetSelIndexBtn);
    }

    public boolean action(Event evt, Object arg)
     {int nIndex;
      String text = (String)arg;
      String str;
```

```
if (evt.target instanceof Button) {

    if (text.equals("Add String")) {
        // get string in String box
        str = m_StringTxt.getText();
        // insert string in list box
        m_NamesLst.addItem(str);
    }
    else if (text.equals("Delete String")) {
        // get index of selected item
        nIndex = m_NamesLst.getSelectedIndex();
        // delete selected item
        m_NamesLst.delItem(nIndex);
        // select next item
        if (m_NamesLst.countItems() > 0) {
            if (nIndex > 0)
                nIndex--;
            m_NamesLst.select(nIndex);
        }
    }
    else if (text.equals("Get Selected String"))
    {
        // store selected item in string
        str = m_NamesLst.getSelectedItem();
        // put string in String Box
        m_StringTxt.setText(str);
    }
    else if (text.equals("Get Selected Index")) {
        // get index of selected item
        nIndex = m_NamesLst.getSelectedIndex();
        // display index in Index Box
        m_IndexTxt.setText("" + nIndex);
    }
}
return true;
}
}
```

This source code contains the declarations and statements of the class UseSingleList that support the list and other controls. The class declares the following attributes:

- ✦ The label object m_ListBoxLbl, which has the text "List Box"

- ✦ The label object m_StringLbl, which has the text "String"

- ✦ The label object m_IndexLbl, which has the text "Index"

- ✦ The single-selection list m_NamesLst, which displays up to five items

- ✦ The edit box object m_StringTxt, which appears near the String label

♦ The edit box object m_IndexTxt, which appears near the Index label

♦ The button object m_AddStrBtn, which has the label Add String

♦ The button object m_DelStrBtn, which has the label Delete String

♦ The button object m_GetSelStrBtn, which has the label Get Selected String

♦ The button object m_GetSelIndexBtn, which has the label Get Selected Index

The next sections discuss the methods of the class UseSingleList.

The method init ( )

The method init() performs the following tasks:

♦ Adds a set of names to the scrolling list. This task sends the message addItem() to the object m_NamesLst to add a name. The argument for the message is the added name.

♦ Adds the list, labels, edit boxes, and buttons to the drawing area.

The method action ( )

The method action() responds to the event that is generated by clicking a button. This method uses an if statement to examine the condition (evt.target instanceof Button) and determine if the event was generated by a button. If this condition is true, the method determines which button generated the event. The following sections describe what happens for each button.

The Add String button

The Add String button causes the program to add the string in the String edit box to the list. The method performs the following tasks:

♦ Stores a copy of the text in the String edit box in the local string variable str. This task sends the message getText() to the object m_StringTxt.

♦ Adds the contents of variable str to the list by sending the message addItem() to that list. The argument for this message is the variable str.

The Delete String button

The Delete String button causes the program to delete the selected item. The method performs the following tasks:

✦ Stores the index of the selected item in the local `int`-type variable `nIndex`. This task sends the message `getSelectedItem()` to the list object `m_NamesLst`.

✦ Deletes the selected list item by sending the message `delItem()` to that list. The argument for this message is the variable `nIndex`.

✦ Selects another item if the list is not empty. This task sends the message `countItems()` to object `m_NamesLst` to obtain the current number of list items. This task also sends the message `select()` to the object `m_NamesLst` to select the item at index `nIndex`.

The Get Selected String button

The Get Selected String button copies the selected list item to the String edit box. The method performs the following tasks:

✦ Stores the selected item in the local variable `str`. This task sends the message `getSelectedItem()` to the list object `m_NamesLst`.

✦ Displays the characters of the variable `str` in the String edit box. This task sends the message `setText()` to that edit box. The argument for this message is the variable `str`.

The Get Selected Index button

The Get Selected Index button displays the index of the selected list items in the Index edit box. The method performs the following tasks:

✦ Stores the index selected item in the local variable `nIndex`. This task sends the message `getSelectedIndex()` to the list object `m_NamesLst`.

✦ Displays the value of the variable `nIndex` in the Index edit box. This task sends the message `setText()` to that edit box. The argument for this message is the expression `""+ nIndex`.

## Part XII

Advanced OOP

This part looks at more advanced topics for novice Java programmers. This part covers creating and using dialog boxes to interact with the end user. In addition, this part presents the AWT classes that manage the layout of controls on a Web page. Finally, this part shows you how to build menu systems and how to respond to them.

In this part

- ✔ Working with dialog boxes
- ✔ Using layout managers
- ✔ Working with menus

Dialog Boxes

The AWT library offers the class `Dialog` to support general dialog boxes. This class allows you to create dialog boxes to display information and accept a user's input. The class `Dialog` supports dialog boxes that can be nonresizable and modal. A *modal* dialog box is one that you must close before you can access any other part of the same application. The class `Dialog` declares a constructor and several methods. The following table shows the constructor and relevant methods of the class `Dialog`:

Constructor/Method	*Purpose*
public Dialog(Frame parent, boolean modal)	Creates a dialog box that is initially invisible. The parameter `parent` specifies the owner of the dialog box. The parameter `modal` specifies whether the dialog box is modal.
public Dialog(Frame parent, String title, boolean modal)	Creates a dialog box that is initially invisible. The parameter `parent` specifies the owner of the dialog box. The parameter `title` defines the title of the dialog box. The parameter `modal` specifies whether the dialog box is modal.
Public String getTitle( )	Returns the title of the dialog box.
public boolean isModal( )	Returns `true` if the dialog box is modal and `false` if it is not.
public boolean isResizable( )	Returns `true` if the dialog box is resizable and `false` if it is not.
public void setResizable (boolean resizable)	Specifies whether the user can resize the dialog box.
public void setTitle(String title)	Sets the new title of the dialog box.

The class `Dialog` and its descendants do not have a default layout scheme. You must specify a layout scheme to make the controls of the dialog box visible.

The following is an example of creating a message dialog box that includes a static text control (which displays a message) and a button labeled `OK`:

```
class myDialog extends Dialog
{
  public myDialog(Frame parent,
                  String title,
                  String message)
  {
    // create dialog box with title
    super(parent, title, true);
```

```
        // set the layout manager
        setLayout(new FlowLayout());
        // add controls
        add(new Label(message));
        add(new Button"OK"));
    }
    ...
}
```

This example declares the class myDialog as a descendant of the
class Dialog. The example shows the constructor of the class,
and the constructor performs the following tasks:

+ Invokes the constructor of the parent class. The arguments for
  this invocation are the Frame-type parameter parent, the title
  of the dialog box, and true (an argument for the parameter
  modal).

+ Sets a layout manager by invoking the method setLayout.
  Without this task, the class displays an empty dialog box.

+ Adds a static text control that displays the message that is
  passed by the String-type parameter message.

+ Adds the button control labeled OK.

The preceding example shows that it's good programming practice
to declare a class for each dialog box that you want to use in an
applet. The class uses its constructor to create the dialog boxes
and offers methods to respond to events that are generated by the
controls in the dialog box. Finally, the class can provide methods
that return data from the controls of the dialog box.

The following programming example uses a dialog box. This
program displays a button labeled Dialog!. When you click this
button, the program displays a modal message dialog box that has
the title Information, the message Please click the OK
button, and a button labeled OK. When you click this button, the
program hides the dialog box. When you click the Dialog! button,
you see the dialog box again, and so on. The following figure
shows a sample session with the dialog box test program.

```
import java.applet.*;
import java.awt.*;

public class UseDialog extends Applet
{
    protected Frame m_frm;
    protected MsgDialog m_db;
    protected Button m_DialogBtn;

public String getAppletInfo()
    {
    return "";
```

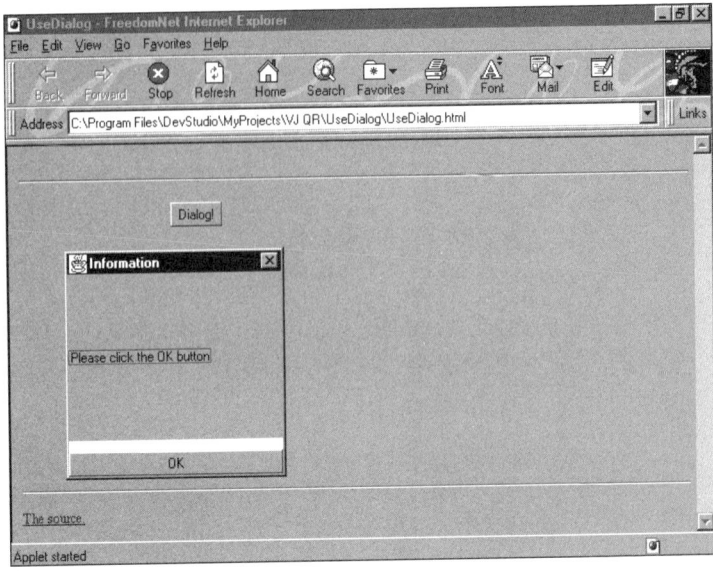

```
    }
public void init()
    {
resize(320, 240);
        // create frame, dialog box, and controls
        m_frm = new Frame();
        m_db = new MsgDialog(m_frm, "Information",
                "Please click the OK button",
    true);
        m_DialogBtn = new Button("Dialog!");


        // set the size of the dialog box
        m_db.resize(200, 200);
        // prevent user from resizing dialog box
        m_db.setResizable(false);

        // add Dialog! button to main frame
        add(m_DialogBtn);
    }
public boolean action(Event evt, Object arg)
    {
        if (evt.target instanceof Button) {
          String text = (String)arg;
          if (text.equals("Dialog!"))
            m_db.show();
    }
        return true;
    }
```

(continued)

(continued)

```
          }

     class MsgDialog extends Dialog
     {
       protected Label m_MsgLbl = new Label();
       protected Button m_OKBtn = new Button("OK");

       public MsgDialog(Frame parent,
                        String title,
                        String message,
                        boolean modal)
       {
         // create dialog box with title
         super(parent, title, modal);
         setLayout(new BorderLayout(10, 10));
         m_MsgLbl.setText(message);
         add("Center", m_MsgLbl);
         add("South", m_OKBtn);
       }

       public boolean action(Event evt, Object arg)
       {
         if (evt.target instanceof Button) {
           String text = (String)arg;
           if (text.equals("OK"))
             hide();
         }
         return true;
       }
     }
```

This code declares the new classes UseDialog and MsgDialog.
The class UseDialog declares the following attributes:

+ The Frame-type attribute m_frm, which provides the frame
  that is associated with the dialog box

+ The MsgDialog-type attribute m_db, which represents the
  message dialog box

+ The Button-type attribute m_DialogBtn, which supports the
  button labeled Dialog!

The next sections discuss the methods of the class UseDialog.

The method init ( )

The method init() performs the following tasks:

+ Creates the frame object that is associated with the attribute
  m_frm.

+ Creates the message dialog box that is associated with the
  attribute m_db. This task creates the dialog box by using the

arguments m_frm, the title Information, the message Please click the OK button, and the modal state. The dialog box is initially hidden.

✦ Creates the button labeled Dialog!.

✦ Sets the dimensions of the dialog box to be 200 pixels in length and 200 pixels in width. This task sends the message resize() to the dialog box. The arguments for this message are 200 and 200.

✦ Adds the Dialog! button to the main frame.

The method action ( )

The method action() responds to the event that is generated by clicking the Dialog! button. This method uses an if statement to examine the condition (evt.target instanceof Button) and determines whether the event was generated by a button. If this condition is true, the method determines that the Dialog! button generated the event. If this condition is false, the method displays the dialog box by sending it the message show().

The class MsgDialog

The source code declares the class MsgDialog as a descendant of the class Dialog. This class has the following attributes:

✦ The Label-type attribute m_MsgLbl, which represents the message that is displayed in the dialog box

✦ The Button-type attribute m_OKBtn, which supports the button that is labeled OK

The class initializes both attributes in their declarations.

The constructor

The class MsgDialog has a constructor with four parameters:

✦ The Frame-type parameter parent refers to the frame that owns the dialog box.

✦ The String-type parameters title and message specify the title and message of the dialog box, respectively.

✦ The boolean-type parameter modal is the modal state flag.

The constructor performs the following tasks:

✦ Invokes the constructor of the parent class. The arguments for this invocation are the Frame-type parameter parent, the title of the dialog box, and the parameter modal.

✦ Sets a layout manager by invoking the method setLayout().
The class uses the border layout scheme by creating a new
instance of the class BorderLayout.

✦ Assigns the text of the message to the static text control.

✦ Adds a static text control to the center of the dialog box. This
task invokes the version of the method add(), which specifies
the navigational direction Center.

✦ Adds the button control labeled OK to the bottom of the dialog
box. This task invokes the version of the method add(),
which specifies the navigational direction South.

The method action ( )

The method action() responds to the event that is generated by
clicking the OK button. The method uses an if statement to
examine the condition (evt.target instanceof Button) and
determine if the event was generated by a button. If this condition
is true, the method determines that the OK button generated the
event. If this condition is false, the method hides the dialog box by
sending it the message hide().

Managing Layouts

The order of showing and placing visual controls on the frame (in
the Web page) depends on two factors: the order of adding the
visual controls and the layout manager that is used. The layout
manager determines which parts of the frame are used to display
which components. The advantage of using layout managers is
that they support creating Web pages that work on different
platforms.

The Java AWT library offers the classes FlowLayout, GridLayout,
GridBagLayout, BorderLayout, and CardLayout to support the
various types of layout managers and schemes. This section
discusses most of these layout managers and shows you sample
output and the code that is related to the output.

To use any layout manager, the AWT library offers the method
setLayout(), which takes a single argument. This argument is one of
the previously mentioned layout manager classes. You typically use
the setLayout() method in the method init() as follows:

```
public void init()
{
  ...
  setLayout(new FlowLayout());
  ...
}
```

This example sets a layout manager by using the FlowLayout class.

The class FlowLayout

The class FlowLayout offers the simplest layout scheme. By default, Java applets use this layout scheme, which arranges the visual controls in rows from left to right. When a row cannot fit another control, the layout manager wraps the control to the next row. By default, the FlowLayout class centers the controls. You can use two of the three constructors to specify the alignment of the controls. The following table shows the constructors of the class FlowLayout:

Constructor	Purpose
public FlowLayout()	Creates a flow layout with centered controls.
public FlowLayout(int align)	Creates a flow layout that aligns the controls by using the value of parameter align (which can have the values LEFT, RIGHT, or CENTER).
public FlowLayout(int align, int hgap, int vgap)	Creates a flow layout that aligns the controls by using the value of the parameter align. The parameters hgap and vgap specify the horizontal and vertical gaps between the controls, respectively.

The following code shows you how to use the three constructors of the class FlowLayout. The subsequent figure is sample output that is generated by using the default constructor of the class FlowLayout as follows:

```
public void init()
{
    ...
    setLayout(new FlowLayout());
    add(new Button("Button 1"));
    add(new Button("Button 2"));
    add(new Button("Button 3"));
    add(new Button("Button 4"));
    add(new Button("Button 5"));
    ...
}
```

This figure shows the five buttons as they appear centered in the drawing area.

The next figure shows the output that is generated by using the second constructor of the class FlowLayout as follows:

```
public void init()
{
    ...
    setLayout(new FlowLayout(FlowLayout.LEFT));
```

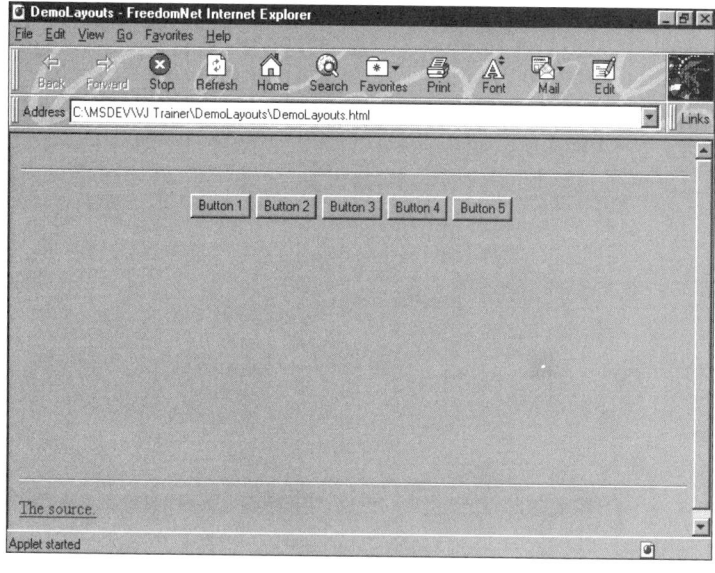

```
add(new Button("Button 1"));
add(new Button("Button 2"));
add(new Button("Button 3"));
add(new Button("Button 4"));
add(new Button("Button 5"));
...
}
```

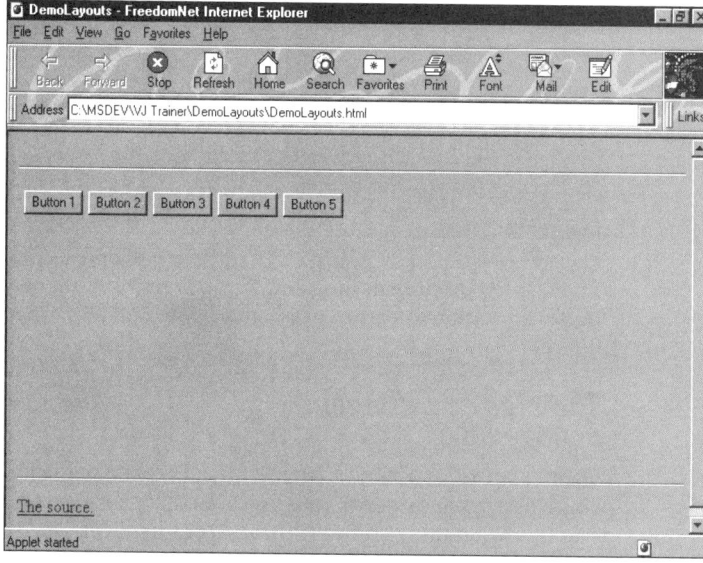

This figure shows the five buttons as they appear left aligned in the drawing area. The argument FlowLayout.LEFT used with the constructor causes these buttons to be aligned to the left.

The next figure shows sample output that is generated by using the third constructor of class FlowLayout as follows:

```
public void init()
{
  ...
  setLayout(new FlowLayout(FlowLayout.LEFT), 20,
    20);
  add(new Button("Button 1"));
  add(new Button("Button 2"));
  add(new Button("Button 3"));
  add(new Button("Button 4"));
  add(new Button("Button 5"));
  ...
}
```

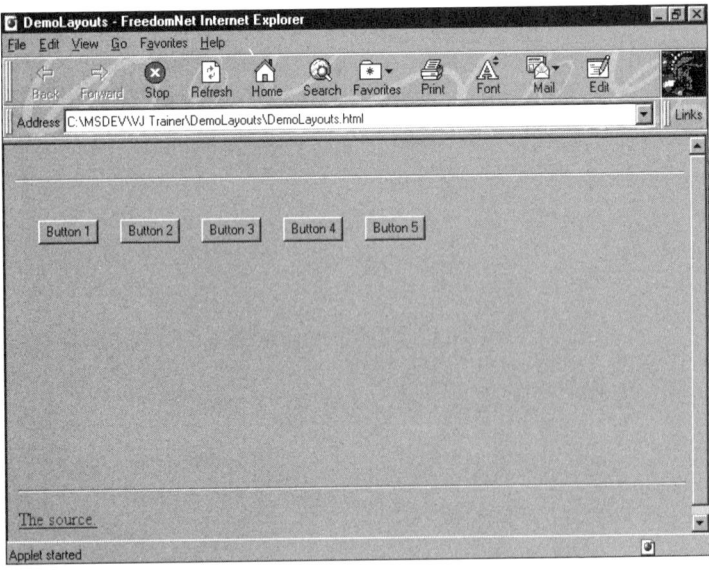

The last two arguments used with the constructor cause these buttons to appear farther apart than they are in the previous two figures.

The class GridLayout

The class GridLayout supports a layout scheme that arranges the visual control as a grid over the drawing area. Typically, the controls appear larger than if you are using the class FlowLayout. The following table shows the constructors of the class GridLayout:

Constructor	Purpose
public GridLayout()	Creates a grid layout that has the controls appearing adjacent to each other in a grid configuration.
public GridLayout(int rows, int cols, int hgap, int vgap)	Creates a grid layout that aligns the controls by using the rows and columns that are specified by parameters rows and cols. The parameters hgap and vgap specify the horizontal and vertical gaps between the controls, respectively.

The following code shows you how to use the two constructors of the class GridLayout. The subsequent figure shows sample output that is generated by using the default constructor of the class GridLayout as follows:

```
public void init()
{
    ...
    setLayout(new GridLayout(3, 3));
    add(new Button("Button 1"));
    add(new Button("Button 2"));
    add(new Button("Button 3"));
    add(new Button("Button 4"));
    add(new Button("Button 5"));
    ...
}
```

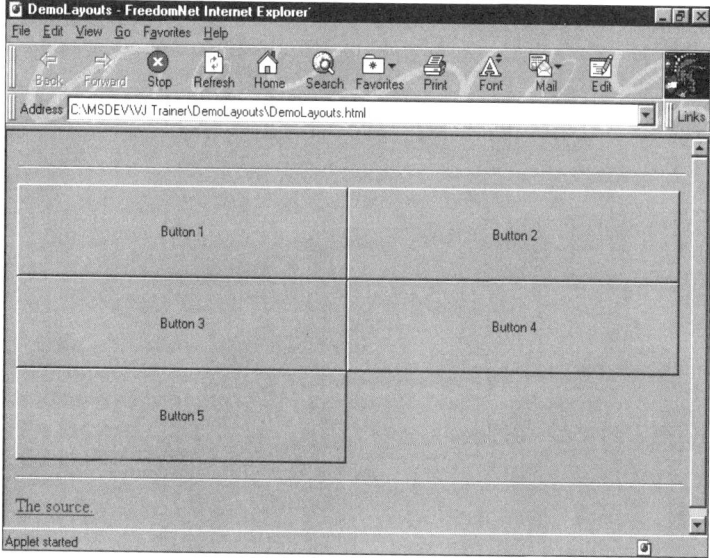

This figure shows the five buttons as they appear in a three-row by three-column grid. Because there are only five buttons, you see only two columns of buttons.

The next figure shows sample output that is generated by using the second constructor of the class GridLayout as follows:

```
public void init()
{
  ...
  setLayout(new GridLayout(3, 3, 10, 15);
  add(new Button("Button 1"));
  add(new Button("Button 2"));
  add(new Button("Button 3"));
  add(new Button("Button 4"));
  add(new Button("Button 5"));
  ...
}
```

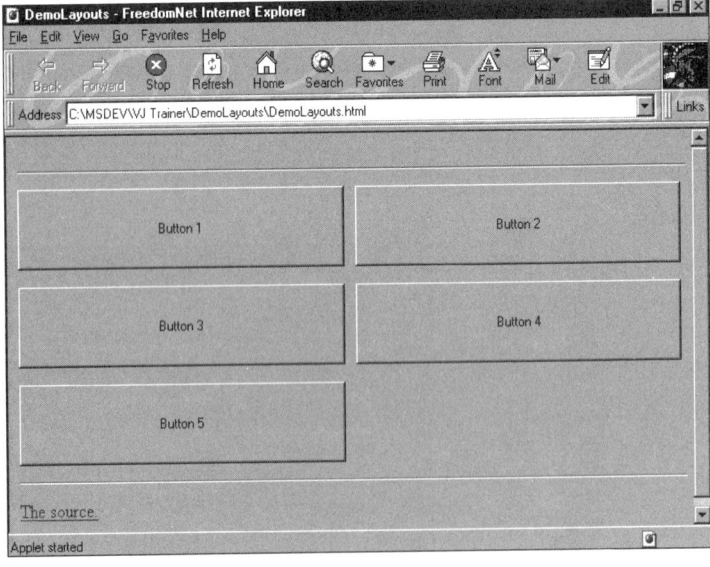

The last two arguments that are used with the constructor cause these buttons to appear with horizontal and vertical gaps of 10 and 15 pixels, respectively.

The class BorderLayout

The class `BorderLayout` supports a scheme that arranges the controls as simple windows. This layout manager places the controls near the edges of the drawing area. You can specify the border to place a control by using the names `"North"`, `"South"`, `"West"`, `"East"`, and `"Center"` to specify the top, bottom, left edge, right edge, and center, respectively. The AWT library provides a special version of the method `add( )` that allows you to specify the edge as the first argument. The following table shows the constructors of the class `BorderLayout`.

Constructor	Purpose
public BorderLayout()	Creates a border layout that displays the controls by using the navigational directions with the method `add( )`.
public BorderLayout(int hgap, int vgap)	Creates a border layout that uses the parameters `hgap` and `vgap` to specify the horizontal and vertical gaps between the controls, respectively.

The classes `GridBagLayout` and `GridBagConstraints` offer a high level of managing the layout of visual controls; however, this topic is beyond the scope of this book.

The following code shows you how to use the two constructors of the class `BorderLayout`. The subsequent figure shows sample output that is generated by using the default constructor of the class `BorderLayout` as follows:

```
public void init()
{
    ...
    setLayout(new BorderLayout());
    add("North", new Button("Button 1"));
    add("South", new Button("Button 2"));
    add("East", new Button("Button 3"));
    add("West", new Button("Button 4"));
    add("Center", new Button("Button 5"));
    ...
}
```

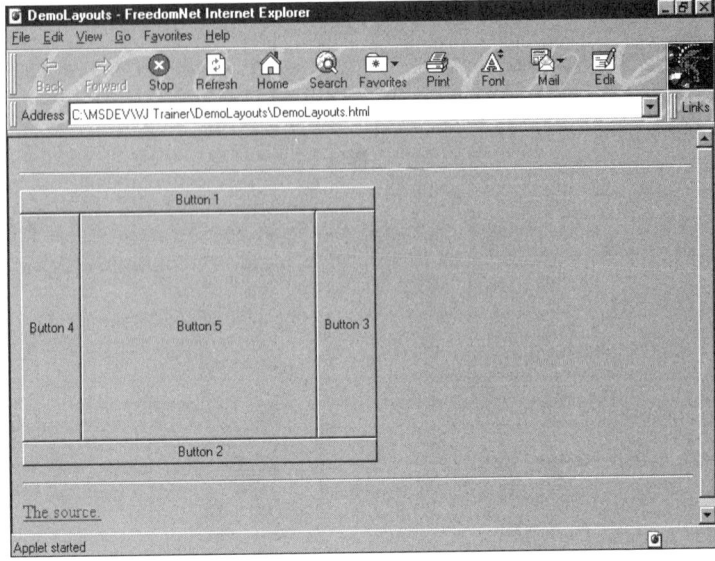

This figure shows the five buttons as they appear using the directional navigation names. Note that the preceding code uses a special version of the method add() to add the controls.

The navigational directions are case sensitive and must be spelled as shown in the preceding code. Otherwise, the add() method ignores the control that you want to insert.

The next figure shows sample output that is generated by using the second constructor of the class BorderLayout as follows:

```
public void init()
{
    ...
    setLayout(new BorderLayout(10, 15));
    add("North", new Button("Button 1"));
    add("South", new Button("Button 2"));
    add("East", new Button("Button 3"));
    add("West", new Button("Button 4"));
    add("Center", new Button("Button 5"));
    ...
}
```

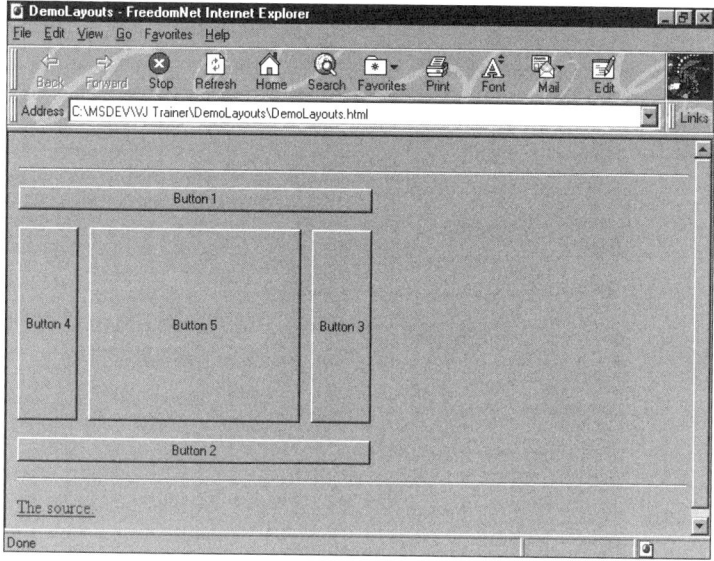

The two arguments that are used with the constructor cause these buttons to appear with a horizontal and vertical gap of 10 and 15 pixels, respectively. The location of the buttons is the same as that in the previous figure.

The class CardLayout

The class CardLayout supports a layout scheme that allows you to display one of several windows, called *panels*. (To this point, I have been using the term *drawing area* in place of the term *panel.*) The AWT library offers the class Panel to represent a drawing area that usually contains visual controls; therefore, every Java applet has at least one panel. Working with panels offers you a sophisticated way of showing and hiding groups of related controls — one group at a time. The class CardLayout works with panels that overlay each other and allows you to select a panel to show at any given time. The following table shows the constructors of the class CardLayout:

Constructor	Purpose
public CardLayout()	Creates a card layout that has multiple panels (or *cards*). Only one panel (or card) appears at a time.
public CardLayout(int hgap, int vgap)	Creates a card layout that uses the parameters hgap and vgap to specify the horizontal and vertical gaps between the cards, respectively. These gaps also shrink the cards by the amount of the gaps.

The following code shows you how to use the two constructors of the class CardLayout. The subsequent figure shows sample output that is generated by using the default constructor of the class CardLayout as follows:

```
public void init()
{
    ...
    CardLayout CL = new CardLayout();
    setLayout(CL);
    // create first panel with "Button 1"
    Panel Panel1 = new Panel();
    Panel1.add(new Button("Button 1"));
    add("one", Panel1);

    // create second panel with "Button 2"
    Panel Panel2 = new Panel();
    Panel2.add(new Button("Button 2"));
    add("two", Panel2);

    // create third panel with "Button 3"
    Panel Panel3 = new Panel();
    Panel3.add(new Button("Button 3"));
    add("three", Panel3);

    // display second panel
    CL.show(this, "two");
    ...
}
```

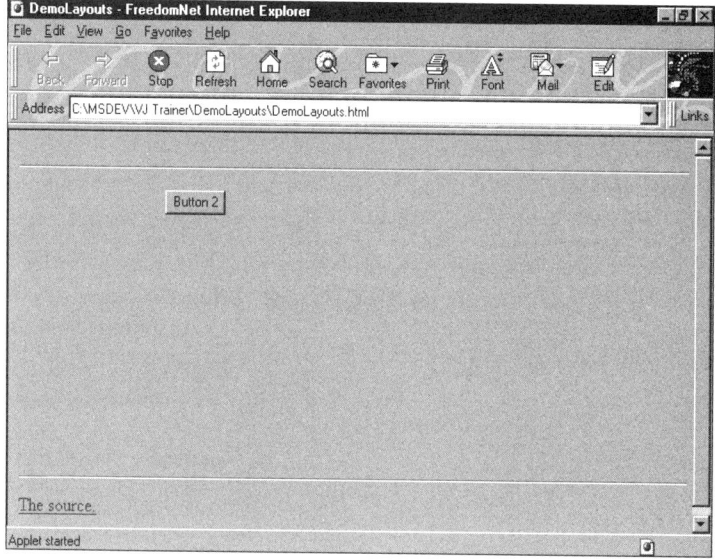

This example performs the following tasks:

+ Creates the object `CL` as an instance of the class `CardLayout`, using the default constructor.

+ Creates the panel `Panel1` as an instance of the class `Panel`.

+ Adds the button labeled `Button 1` to the panel `Panel1`.

+ Adds the panel `Panel1` to the frame. This task uses a special version of the method `add()` that has two arguments. The first one is the name of the panel (`Panel1`), and the second is the panel object itself.

+ Creates the panel `Panel2` as an instance of the class `Panel`.

+ Adds the button labeled `Button 2` to the panel `Panel2`.

+ Adds the panel `Panel2` to the frame. This task uses a special version of the method `add()` that has two arguments. The first one is the name of the panel (`Panel2`), and the second is the panel object itself.

+ Creates the panel `Panel3` as an instance of the class `Panel`.

+ Adds the button labeled `Button 3` to the panel `Panel3`.

+ Adds the panel `Panel3` to the frame. This task uses a special version of the method `add()` that has two arguments. The first one is the name of the panel (`Panel3`), and the second is the panel object itself.

✦ Displays the second panel by sending the message show() to the object CL. The arguments for this message are the reference to the frame, this, and the name of the selected panel. This task causes the second panel with its single button labeled Button 2.

Menu Bars

The menu bar contains the menus and the menu items. The class MenuBar supports the menu bar. This class offers a constructor and a number of methods. The following table shows the constructor and the relevant methods.

Constructor/Method	Purpose
MenuBar()	Creates a menu bar. The constructor does not automatically associate a menu bar with a frame window. You need to use the frame window's setMenuBar() method for that task.
public synchronized Menu add(Menu aMenu)	Adds a menu to the menu bar. Without using this method, a frame displays an empty menu bar.
public int countMenus()	Returns the number of menus in the menu bar.
public Menu getMenu(int index)	Accesses a menu in the menu bar by specifying the menu's position. The first menu is at position 0.
public synchronized void remove(int index)	Removes a menu from the menu bar by specifying the menu's position. The first menu is at position 0.

The key word *synchronized,* when related to a method, indicates that the method performs object management related to threads (multitasking).

The following code shows a general example for creating a menu bar and associating it with a frame window:

```
MyFrame(String title)
{
    ...
    // declare menu bar as an attribute
    MenuBar myBar;
    // create a new menu bar
    myBar = new MenuBar();
    // associate menu bar with the frame
    setMenubar(myBar);
    ...
}
```

This example declares and creates the menu bar `myBar` and then attaches it to the frame. The latter task involves sending the message `setMenuBar()` to the frame window. The parameter for this message is the menu bar object `myBar`.

Menu Items

After you create an empty menu bar, you need to insert at least one menu in it. The class `Menu` supports the menus that appear in the menu bar. This class offers a constructor and a number of methods. The following table shows the constructor and its relevant methods.

Constructor/Method	Purpose
Menu(String label)	Creates a menu with the text that is specified by the parameter label. The constructor does not automatically associate a menu bar with a frame window. You need to use the frame window's setMenuBar() method for that task.
public synchronized MenuItem add(MenuItem aMenuItem)	Adds a menu item to the menu. Without using this method, a frame displays a menu with no pull-down menu items.
public int countItems()	Returns the number of menu items in a menu.
public MenuItem getItem(int index)	Accesses a menu item by specifying the item's position. The first menu item is at position 0.
public synchronized void item's remove(int index)	Removes a menu item by specifying the position. The first menu item is at position 0.
public void addSeparator()	Adds a separator line to the bottom of a menu item at its current position.

The following code shows a general example of creating a menu bar, inserting a menu in the menu bar, and then associating the menu bar with a frame window:

```
MyFrame(String title)
{
    ...
    // declare menu bar as an attribute
    MenuBar myBar;
    // create a new menu bar
    myBar = new MenuBar();
    // create a new menu
```

(continued)

(continued)

```
Menu theFileMenu = new Menu("&File");
// insert menu in the bar
myBar.add(theFileMenu);
// associate menu bar with the frame
setMenubar(myBar);
...
}
```

This code builds on the example in the previous section by declaring and creating the menu theFileMenu (which has the label "&File") and then adding it to the menu bar object myBar. This task involves sending the message add() to the menu bar object. The argument for this message is the menu theFileMenu.

The example shows that the label includes the & character, which specifies the hot key. In the case of the preceding example, the menu has the letter F as the hot key.

Note that the code inserts the menu in the menu bar before the menu is attached to the frame window.

Techie Talk

Applet: There are two basic types of Java programs: applets and applications. You can run an applet in an HTML page when that page is loaded by a Java-capable browser, such as Internet Explorer.

Argument: The value that is assigned to a parameter when you call a function or a member function.

Array: A special variable that stores multiple values.

Array element: A single value in an array that is accessed using one or more indices.

ASCIIZ: A string that stores readable characters and ends with a null character.

Base class: A class that is not a descendant of any other classes.

Bit: Short for binary digit, which is either 0 or 1.

Bitwise: Related to an operation on the individual bits of a value. For example, the bitwise AND operator (the character |) processes the corresponding bits of the two values supplied to that operator.

Boolean expression: An expression that evaluates to either true or false.

Casting: Changing the data type of a value from one type to another compatible type. For example, you can cast an integer into a floating-point value.

Catch: Responding to a run-time error (exception).

Class: A special kind of user-defined type that represents the attributes and operations of a category of objects. A class typically contains attributes and methods.

Class hierarchy: A family of classes in which some or most classes derive from one or more parent classes.

Class instance: An object that is an example of a class.

Class variable: Same as an attribute of a class. This is a term used by other Java books.

Compiler: A program that examines your source code and converts it into an intermediate binary file. The linker converts this intermediate form into an execute file.

Condition: A logical expression.

Console application: An application that runs in a DOS box. This kind of application displays only text and accepts input only from the keyboard.

Constant: A name that is associated with a value that remains fixed during program execution.

Constructor: A special member function that initializes a class instance. Java supports default, copy, and custom constructors.

Copy constructor: A constructor that creates a new instance using the values in an existing one.

Custom constructor: A constructor that is neither a default nor a copy constructor.

Data member: Same as the attribute in a class. This term is used by some authors who by choice use terms inherited from C++.

Data type: A kind of information.

Deallocate: Remove a dynamic variable or array from memory.

Decision-making: The ability to examine a condition and take action.

Default constructor: A constructor with no parameters or with parameters that all have default arguments. Also called a *void constructor.*

Descendant class: A class that is created as a child of another class.

do-while loop: A loop that iterates while a condition is true.

Dynamic array: An array whose size is determined either after its declaration or using the number of elements to initialize it.

Dynamic variable: A variable, structure, or object that is created at runtime using the operator new.

Encapsulate: Include and combine the attributes and the methods to create a class.

Exception: An error that occurs during program execution.

Expression: A collection of operators and values that yields a single result.

Floating-point number: A number with a fractional part.

for loop: A loop that typically iterates for a fixed number of times.

Garbage collection: A feature in a programming language that automatically reclaims dynamic variables when they reach the end of their scope.

GUI: Graphical User Interface. This terms refers to the kind of application, such as Windows 95 and Internet Web pages, that use high-resolution graphics to interact with the user.

Identifier: A name of a program component.

if statement: A decision-making statement that supports single, dual, or multiple alternatives (by nesting if statements).

Instance: See *class instance.*

Logical error: An error that causes the program to do what you tell it do to but not what you want it to do.

Loop: A program part that allows you to repeat one or more tasks.

Member function: Same as a method in a class. This is a term used by Java book authors who choose to use terms inherited from C++.

Message: The invocation of a method with a specific class instance.

Method overloading: Using the same name to declare multiple methods, each with a unique parameter list.

Multiple inheritance: A scheme for creating a class hierarchy where a descendant class has two or more parent classes. Java does not support multiple inheritance.

Multithreading: Simultaneously running several copies of parts of an application or applet.

Object: An instance of a class.

Operator: A symbol or name that takes a value and yields a result.

Parameter: A special variable that passes information from (and often to) a method.

Recursive method: A method that calls itself.

Runtime error: An error that occurs when the program attempts to perform an illegal task, such as reading from a nonexistent file.

Send a message: Invoke a method with a specific class instance.

Single inheritance: A scheme for creating a class hierarchy where each descendant class has only one parent class.

Static member: A class attribute that conceptually belongs to the class itself instead of any class instance.

String: A set of characters that store text.

String class: A Java class that supports strings.

Switch statement: A decision-making statement that supports multiple alternatives.

Throw: Raising a runtime error (exception).

Variable: A name that is associated with a value that can change during program execution.

Void constructor: A constructor with no parameters. Also called a *default constructor.*

while loop: A loop that iterates as long as a condition is true.

Index

Symbols

A

B

(continued)

IDG BOOKS WORLDWIDE REGISTRATION CARD

Visit our Web site at http://www.idgbooks.com

ISBN Number: 0-7645-0253-0

Title of this book: Visual J++ For Dummies, QR

IDG BOOKS WORLDWIDE
THE WORLD OF COMPUTER KNOWLEDGE®

My overall rating of this book: ❏ Very good [1] ❏ Good [2] ❏ Satisfactory [3] ❏ Fair [4] ❏ Poor [5]

How I first heard about this book:

❏ Found in bookstore; name: [6]

❏ Book review: [7]

❏ Advertisement: [8]

❏ Catalog: [9]

❏ Word of mouth; heard about book from friend, co-worker, etc.: [10]

❏ Other: [11]

What I liked most about this book:

What I would change, add, delete, etc., in future editions of this book:

Other comments:

Number of computer books I purchase in a year: ❏ 1 [12] ❏ 2-5 [13] ❏ 6-10 [14] ❏ More than 10 [15]

I would characterize my computer skills as: ❏ Beginner [16] ❏ Intermediate [17] ❏ Advanced [18] ❏ Professional [19]

I use ❏ DOS [20] ❏ Windows [21] ❏ OS/2 [22] ❏ Unix [23] ❏ Macintosh [24] ❏ Other: [25]_____ (please specify)

I would be interested in new books on the following subjects:

(please check all that apply, and use the spaces provided to identify specific software)

❏ Word processing: [26] | ❏ Spreadsheets: [27]

❏ Data bases: [28] | ❏ Desktop publishing: [29]

❏ File Utilities: [30] | ❏ Money management: [31]

❏ Networking: [32] | ❏ Programming languages: [33]

❏ Other: [34]

I use a PC at (please check all that apply): ❏ home [35] ❏ work [36] ❏ school [37] ❏ other: [38] _____

The disks I prefer to use are ❏ 5.25 [39] ❏ 3.5 [40] ❏ other: [41]_____

I have a CD ROM: ❏ yes [42] ❏ no [43]

I plan to buy or upgrade computer hardware this year: ❏ yes [44] ❏ no [45]

I plan to buy or upgrade computer software this year: ❏ yes [46] ❏ no [47]

Name: _____ Business title: [48] _____

Type of Business: [49]

Address (❏ home [50] ❏ work [51]/Company name: _____

Street/Suite#

City [52]/State [53]/Zip code [54]: _____ Country [55] _____

❏ **I liked this book!**
You may quote me by name in future IDG Books Worldwide promotional materials.
My daytime phone number is _____

❏ YES!

Please keep me informed about IDG Books Worldwide's
World of Computer Knowledge. Send me your latest catalog.